Savoring the
WINE COUNTRY

Savoring the
WINE COUNTRY

Recipes from the Finest Restaurants of Northern California's Wine Regions

Compiled and edited by Meesha Halm and Dayna Macy

Photography by Steven Rothfeld

Introduction by Antonia Allegra

CollinsPublishersSanFrancisco

A Division of HarperCollinsPublishers

First published in USA 1995 by Collins Publishers San Francisco

Copyright © 1995 by Collins Publishers San Francisco

Photography copyright © 1995 by Steven Rothfeld

Art Direction and Design: Kari Perin

Map: Tony Morse

Library of Congress Cataloging-in-Publication Data

Halm, Meesha.

Savoring the Wine Country: recipes from the finest restaurants of northern

California's wine regions/compiled and edited by Meesha Halm and Dayna Macy;

photography by Steven Rothfeld; introduction by Antonia Allegra.

p. cm.

Includes index.

ISBN 0-00-638287-8

1. Cookery, American--California style. 2. Restaurants--California--Napa--Guidebooks.

3. Restaurants--California--Sonoma--Guidebooks. 4. Restaurants--California--Mendocino--Guidebooks. 5. Wine lists.

I. Macy, Dayna. II. Title.

TX715.2.C34H35 1995

641.59794--dc20 CIP 94-30073

Printed in Italy 10 9 8 7 6 5 4 3 2 1

ACKNOWLEDGMENTS

Creating a book is much like preparing a fine meal. There are so many people behind the scenes who help create it, and yet all the recipient sees is the final product. We would like to thank all the participating chefs who generously contributed their time and recipes to the book, not only those whose names appear on these pages, but also the sous chefs, line cooks, pastry chefs, front-of-the-house sorts, and administrators.

Thanks also to everyone who collaborated with us on the content of the book. We'd especially like to thank Antonia Allegra, who welcomed us into valley life, for her friendship and for her historical insight into the regions. Also to Thom Elkjer, for his help crafting the narrative, Frances Bowles, for shepherding the manuscript from a collection of chefs' recipes to a cohesive cookbook, Linda Carucci and Suzy Farnsworth, for their meticulous recipe testing, and Caroline Cory, for her editorial assistance.

Our heartfelt gratitude goes to all our family and friends who supported us throughout this project, especially Jon Fox, Scott Rosenberg, Beverly and Jerry Halm, Estelle Macy, Julie Mautner, Jean and Coleman Rosenberg, and Laurie Wagner. We would also like to express thanks to our co-workers at Collins Publishers, especially Jennifer Barry, Maura Carey Damacion, and Clayton Carlson.

Finally to Kari Perin, for her art direction and Stephen Rothfeld, for his incredible eye, who together translated our vision into this beautiful book.

The art director and photographer wish to thank all the chefs and their staffs for their help in the creation of the photographs and express sincere gratitude to the following individuals and places for their generous hospitality: Albion River Inn, Auberge du Soleil, Laura Chenel, Robert Curry, Fred Halpert, Marsha Huber, Donna and Giovanni Scala, Ellyn Stein, St. Orres, Karen Waikiki, and Sherry Yard. Thank you Charles Gautreaux of Vanderbilt and Company and Paul Stokey of Tesoro for your help with the cover and Armstrong Ranch in Calistoga for the backdrop of exquisite vineyards. Thanks to Gregg Perin for your wheels, Milan for being born just before the photography began, and Susan Swan and Marika for their patient help with the location scouting. Finally, thanks to Jennifer Barry for encouraging our collaboration and sharing the vision.

Preface

Napa, Sonoma, and Mendocino counties, collectively known as California's wine country, are already famous for producing some of the world's premier wines. Now the region is sparking a culinary revolution as well. The combination of great wine, glorious produce, and an influx of talented, visionary chefs has produced some of the finest world-class restaurants, on par with the best in San Francisco, Paris, and New York. But there's one difference: The chefs of the wine country cook what is grown in their own backyards. They are inspired by the earth they stand on, and their food expresses this inspiration.

Within these pages you will meet some of the most creative chefs anywhere, whose enviable task is to create dishes with locally grown produce and locally vinted wine. Our criterion for their inclusion is simple: that they serve the best food the region has to offer. These restaurants are a diverse representation of wine-country cooking—they vary from fancy to funky, classic French to all-American. The list of contributing restaurants was limited only by the number of pages available.

Each restaurant has provided a full three-course menu with recommendations for wine. The recipes range from simple to complex and have been tested for the home chef. We encourage you to try them at your own pace. Make the entire meal or just one course; try the wines recommended or experiment with your own pairings. We've also included two bakeries: In addition to great desserts, great bread is an integral part of wine-country dining—you'll often find it on the table next to a saucer of olive oil.

The restaurants are arranged in geographical order from Napa to Sonoma to Mendocino counties, much the way a visitor setting out from San Francisco would travel through the region. Beginning at the southern end of the wine country in the town of Napa, our culinary journey moves up Highway 29 before jumping over to the Silverado Trail and up to Calistoga. Then we jog east to Sonoma County, along its main thoroughfares, Highways 101 and 128, where the sprawling rolling hills of vineyards and poultry ranches offer a contrast with the more densely populated, narrow enclave of Napa. Finally, we travel up the north coast and toward the Pacific Ocean to Mendocino County, passing through the sleepy towns of Boonville and Gualala along the winding Highway 1 to the town of Mendocino. The food and sensibilities of these regions vary as dramatically as the land, and yet they all offer some of the greatest dining experiences to be found anywhere in the world.

Somehow, the experience of traveling through the wine country is greater than any written summary can suggest. The ever-changing landscape is breathtaking, the repetition of rolling fields of grapevines is mesmerizing. The produce is delicious, the wine outstanding. It's hard to imagine that such a beautiful place exists. Visiting here is more than tasting the wine and eating the food— it is an opportunity to reconnect with the earth. This intimate experience of seeing where our food comes from can bring the visitor not only a greater appreciation of eating, but also a sense of inner peace.

Savoring the Wine Country is a slice of wine-country life at this moment in time. New restaurants will open, others might close; a chef might move to another restaurant; your favorite dish may come off the menu. It's all a part of a creative, dynamic, and evolving scene. The visions and stories of the chefs are the collective voice of the book, and they speak for themselves. We invite you to experience, taste, and relish the food of the wine country, whether you are savoring it in a vineyard or recreating it in your home.

TABLE OF CONTENTS

Introduction　　　　　　　　　　　　　　　　　9
NAPA COUNTY

Bistro Don Giovanni　　　　　　　　　　　　16
　Comice Pear and Stilton Salad
　Braised Lamb Shanks with White Beans
　Chocolate-Polenta Mousse Cake

Domaine Chandon Restaurant　　　　　　20
　Smoked Red Trout Marinated in Olive Oil
　Sea Bass with Lentils and Mashed Potatoes
　Pear, Banana and Chocolate Sorbets

Mustards Grill　　　　　　　　　　　　　　24
　Grilled Stuffed Pasilla Peppers with Tomatillo Salsa
　Grilled Skirt Steak with Pepper Catsup
　Jack Daniels Chocolate Cake

Stars Oakville Café　　　　　　　　　　　　30
　Pumpkin-Filled Pasta Gratin with Roast Fennel
　Red Wine–Braised Beef Cheeks with Root Vegetable Purée
　　and Braised Red Onions
　Baked Apple Caramel with Berry Sauce

Auberge du Soleil　　　　　　　　　　　　34
　Goat Cheese Tartlets
　Ahi and Salmon Tempura Sushi
　Warm Cappuccino Bread Pudding with Caramel Sauce

The Restaurant at Meadowood　　　　　38
　Warm Calamari with White Bean Vinaigrette
　Medallions of Lamb Wrapped in Red Onion
　Poached Pears with Cinnamon and Vanilla Risotto

Tra Vigne Ristorante　　　　　　　　　　42
　Goat Cheese Salad with Oven-Dried Figs
　Chicken Breast with Potato and Pea Risotto
　Torta Sabiosa

Terra　　　　　　　　　　　　　　　　　46
　Tataki of Tuna with Field Greens
　　and Mustard-Soy Vinaigrette
　Grilled Salmon with Cabbage, Thai Red Curry Sauce
　　and Basmati Rice
　Sautéed Strawberries in Cabernet Sauvignon
　　and Black Pepper Sauce

The Model Bakery　　　　　　　　　　　　50
　Turtle Cake
　Walnut Bread

Brava Terrace　　　　　　　　　　　　　　54
　Provençal Salad with Marinated Goat Cheese
　Cassoulet of Lentils with Chicken, Sausage and Pork
　Fresh Fruit with English Cream and Mint

All Seasons Café and Wine Shop　　　　58
　Field Greens with Brazil Nut Oil Vinaigrette
　Breast of Duck with Huckleberry Sauce
　　and Wild Rice Yam Cakes
　Flourless Chocolate Coconut Cake

Catahoula Restaurant and Saloon　　　62
　Soft-Shell Crabs with Vegetable Slaw and Rémoulade
　Warm Roasted Rabbit and White Bean Salad
　　with Tomato Confit
　Mango and Blackberry Upside-Down Cake

SONOMA COUNTY

Ristorante Piatti　　　　　　　　　　　　68
　Involtini with Goat Cheese and Basil
　Pasta Siciliana
　Poached Pears with Caramel Sauce, Vanilla Gelato
　　and Almond Cookies

Eastside Oyster Bar and Grill　　　　　72
　Eastside's Hangtown Fry
　Spiced, Smoked and Grilled Pork Loin with Tomatillo
　　and Chayote Salsa and Soft Polenta
　Santa Rosa Plum Tart with Brandy 'n' Spice Ice Cream

The Grille at the Sonoma Mission Inn and Spa　　76
　Wild Mushroom Bruschetta
　Seared New York Strip with Foie Gras
　　and Garlic Mashed Potatoes
　Warm Chocolate Waffles with Ice Cream
　　and Raspberry Sauce

Kenwood Restaurant and Bar ... 80
  Gazpacho
  Peppered Tuna with Papaya
  Figs with Raspberry Coulis and Mint

Willowside Café ... 84
  Halibut in Corn Crêpes with Tomato Coulis
  Roast Duck Lasagne with Greens and Sage
  Fig and Raspberry Gratin with Praline Cookies

John Ash and Company ... 88
  Crab Cakes with Cabbage Slaw
    and Blood Orange Mayonnaise
  Squab Braised in Cider
  Almond Orange Tart with Ginger Crème Anglaise

Samba Java ... 92
  Spicy Coconut and Pumpkin Soup
  Chinese Black Bean Spareribs with Confetti Slaw
    and Fried Plantains
  Ginger Crème Brûlée

Bistro Ralph ... 96
  Anise-Flavored Focaccine
  Braised Chilean Sea Bass
  Chocolate Pâté

Downtown Bakery and Creamery ... 100
  Apple Polenta Tart
  Blueberry Scones

Madrona Manor ... 102
  Duck Confit Agnolotti with Fall Squash Sauce
    and Lemon Cream
  Veal Loin with a Medley of Peppers, Black Bean Purée
    and Corn Salsa
  Apricot Soufflés in Phyllo Pastry on a Palette
    of Fruit Sauces

Chateau Souverain – Cafe at the Winery ... 106
  Leek and Potato Soup with Anise
  Roasted Sonoma Chicken with Vegetable Couscous
  Almond Shortcake with Seasonal Berries

MENDOCINO COUNTY

The Boonville Hotel ... 112
  Roasted Vegetable Bisque with Thyme
  Roast Pork Loin in Red Chile and Oregano
    with Soft Polenta
  Cranberry Kuchen with Hot Cream Sauce

St. Orres ... 118
  Seafood with Saffron Pasta and Seaweed
  Wild Mushroom–Stuffed Quail with Sweet Yam Waffles
  Wild Huckleberry Tart

The Ledford House Restaurant ... 122
  Gravlax of Halibut with Citrus Vinaigrette
  Grilled Salmon with Avocado Butter and Fried Sage
  Chocolate Truffle Torte with Raspberry Purée
    and Chantilly Cream

Albion River Inn ... 126
  Sesame-Seared Sea Scallops with Risotto and
    Orange-Riesling Sauce
  House-Smoked Pork Loin with Huckleberry Sauce
    and Wild Rice and Pasta Medley
  Apple-Crumb Cobbler with Vanilla-Bean Ice Cream

Cafe Beaujolais ... 130
  Maple-Glazed Chestnut and Wild Mushroom Ragout
  Pan Roasted Halibut with Soupy White Beans
    and Wilted Kale
  Caramelized Apple Clafoutis with Calvados

955 Ukiah Street Restaurant ... 134
  Roasted White Corn and Red Beet Soup
  Poached Salmon with Tomato and Tarragon Sauce
  Mango Mousse with Huckleberry Sauce

Directory of Restaurants ... 138

Metric Conversion Table ... 139

Index ... 140

1 BISTRO DON GIOVANNI
2 DOMAINE CHANDON RESTAURANT
3 MUSTARDS GRILL
4 STARS OAKVILLE CAFE
5 AUBERGE DE SOLEIL
6 THE RESTAURANT AT MEADOWOOD
7 TRA VIGNE RISTORANTE
8 TERRA
9 THE MODEL BAKERY
10 BRAVA TERRACE
11 ALL SEASONS CAFE AND WINE SHOP
12 CATAHOULA RESTAURANT AND SALOON
13 RISTORANTE PIATTI
14 EASTSIDE OYSTER BAR AND GRILL
15 THE GRILL AT SONOMA MISSION INN AND SPA
16 KENWOOD RESTAURANT AND BAR
17 WILLOWSIDE CAFE
18 JOHN ASH AND COMPANY
19 SAMBA JAVA
20 BISTRO RALPH
21 DOWNTOWN BAKERY AND CREAMERY
22 MADRONA MANOR
23 CHATEAU SOUVERAIN- CAFE AT THE WINERY
24 THE BOONVILLE HOTEL
25 ST. ORRES
26 THE LEDFORD HOUSE RESTAURANT
27 ALBION RIVER INN
28 CAFE BEAUJOLAIS
29 955 UKIAH STREET RESTAURANT

8

Introduction

When my four sisters and I were growing up in San Francisco, Napa Valley meant only two things to us: fried chicken and root beer. In the fifties, we enjoyed Sunday outings with our grandmother to the then-undeveloped California wine country. As we drove along Highway 29 in her navy blue Brougham, she dropped the names of the de Latours, the Beringer boys, and other families that had been prominent before Prohibition, when there were fewer than seventeen active wineries in the valley. After visits to the Calistoga geyser (for us children) and Beringer and Martini (for Grandma), she would choose a grassy spot off the side of the road for a picnic. The perfectly fried chicken was heaped on a white china platter. Cool fresh radishes and peaches from farm stands along the way filled out our meals. The five granddaughters drank root beer, and with her chicken, Grandma drank wine.

Until relatively recently, visitors to the wine country came to taste vintages and stock up on cases of their favorite Chardonnays, Cabernets, and other varietals. But then they would have to settle down for a picnic, like the picnics of my past, or head elsewhere for a restaurant meal. Today, the culinary landscape has been transformed.

From my porch in St. Helena, toward the northern end of the Napa Valley, I can see a hint of the pass in the crest of the Vaca Range that marks the eastern boundary of what northern Californians call the wine country. I love to drive from Napa to Sonoma and Mendocino counties, just to see the geographical changes.

Napa, long and lean on the map, is hugged by mountains on both sides. Only five miles wide and thirty miles long, it is a perfect basin for the vineyards that line the valley from its southern tip in foggy Carneros near the San Francisco Bay to the dormant volcanic terrain of northern Calistoga.

Though it may seem strange, the rockiness of the soil is revered up and down the valley. Vine roots go down as deep as thirty feet and prefer rocky, not fertile, soil.

Like the rest of the wine-growing region, Napa is rich in both natural resources and agriculture. Raspberries, walnuts, pears, herbs, and cherries are widely cultivated and are available at local farmers' markets during the summer and fall. Napa's agricultural specialties, beyond the famous wine grapes, include the orchards of persimmons, peaches, and other fruits that thrived as the chief crops here until the turn of the century and that still line riverbed acreage in the valley.

Paralleling the Napa Valley is the Sonoma Valley—more fertile than its neighbor and far more extensive. Sonoma sprawls from the Mayacamas Range, which separates the two valleys, all the way out to the Pacific Ocean, and it embraces a range of microclimates and soils, offering sinuous mountain roads lined with ancient oaks and redwood trees as well as broad, generous rolling hills. Flowing through Sonoma's interior is the Russian River, which irrigates the soil, yielding perfect growing conditions for fruits and vegetables.

Figs, raspberries, prunes, peaches, pears, lettuces, tomatoes, asparagus, and avocados grow abundantly. With plenty of room for ranching, cattle, pigs, sheep, and goats as well as poultry all thrive, allowing Sonoma to make a name for itself with cheeses as well. Sonoma goat cheese rivals tangy French chèvres and sturdy chunks of local, Italian-style pecorino are favorites at the farmers' markets.

Beyond Sonoma and through the Anderson Valley, Mendocino County lies along the Pacific coast with a cooler and damper climate than the other two regions. The coastline is dotted with Russian Orthodox churches, angular buildings, and seaport towns such as Mendocino itself—which resembles a New England fishing village.

From the battered cliffs of Mendocino County come choice mussels and sea urchins; the ocean provides sablefish, swordfish, Petrale sole, Dungeness crab, and Chinook salmon. Apples, pears, chestnuts, apricots, pistachios, and more produce than you might expect also grow here.

Grapes have been cultivated in these regions since before the Civil War. Father José Altimira's mission in Sonoma included a vineyard as early as 1830, and George C. Yount planted the first grape rootstock in the Napa Valley in 1838, little realizing that he was creating the eventual raison d'être for the valley. In recent years, as California continues to enjoy a growing acceptance and popularity as a world-class wine producer, orchards on the Napa Valley floor have been uprooted to make room for grapes, now the chief crop of that county and one of the major crops of Sonoma and Mendocino.

Popular grape varietals grown in all three valleys include Chardonnay, Sauvignon Blanc, Riesling, Pinot Noir, Cabernet Sauvignon, Zinfandel, and Sangiovese. Napa and Sonoma also grow Merlot, Gewürztraminer, Barbera and Pinot Blanc. Lesser-known grapes, such as Mourvèdre, Carigane, and Viognier, are now being cultivated to blend with the more established varietals.

Seventy-five years ago, Prohibition brought a halt to most winemaking in California, but grape growers survived by producing sacramental and so-called medicinal wines and by shipping most of their fruit out of state to home wine-makers. It wasn't until the winemaking renaissance began during the midsixties, led by Robert Mondavi, Jack and Jamie Davies, and a few other winery owners, that visitors began to arrive in the wine country to taste the new California wines and learn more about modern winemaking.

Those visitors were lucky to find an occasional coffee shop or a hot-dog stand along the way. But the California wine-country food movement as we know it today was already beginning—behind the scenes and in home kitchens. Between the early sixties and the late seventies, recipes from the wine country were published by the San Francisco-based Wine Institute and in the pages of Sunset magazine. For years, those recipe collections, which offered wine and food pairing charts as well as wine-based recipes chiefly from winemakers and their spouses, were the primary source for elaborate winemakers' dinners. Meanwhile, some wineries, such as Trefethen Vineyards and Robert Mondavi Winery, began offering cooking

classes for home cooks interested in "cooking to wine," that is, understanding a wine first and then designing food to complement it.

It took a French company, though, to notice that good food was also important to the visitors to the region. The opening of the elegant restaurant at the Domaine Chandon winery in Yountville in 1977 marked the beginning of a dramatic change in the wine-country dining scene.

This emerging wine-country cooking style was essentially California cuisine—an imaginative blending of techniques and ingredients that are locally grown but trace their origins from around the globe. The ingredients may sound exotic—aubergines, bean-thread noodles, jicama, sea urchins, venison—but they are produced right here; the techniques ranging from those of provincial French cooking to traditional Japanese cuisine have become commonplace here because they reflect the myriad European and other ethnic influences on everyday life in California.

But wine-country cuisine takes the California concept one step further: it combines regional foods using classical and international techniques with regional wines, thereby promoting a strong bond between the chefs and the winemakers.

Many talented chefs were instrumental in the evolution of good food in the wine country. It was Udo Nechutnys, a protégé of the French chef Paul Bocuse, who proved that Napa had first-class food at the restaurant at Domaine Chandon. Mark Dierkheising—a longtime veteran of the region—became known for his creative uses of game and organic produce at his family's two restaurants: the Silverado Tavern, opened in 1976, and All Seasons Cafe, which opened in 1990. The noted chef and cooking teacher Madeleine Kamman moved to the Napa Valley in 1988 and established a school at Beringer Vineyards to teach professional chefs her blend of French and

Californian cooking. Most recently, in 1995, The Culinary Institute of America, the paragon of cooking schools in the United States, opened a branch in the Napa Valley.

Sonoma's culinary development has been more recent than Napa's. Even so, it has generated equally talented chefs and now boasts a number of fine restaurants, many offering food that is in keeping with the more rustic tenor of the region. Gary Danko, now the executive chef at the Ritz-Carlton in San Francisco, transformed Sonoma's first restaurant at a winery, Chateau Souverain, into a culinary destination during his tenure between 1986 to 1991. Charles Saunders made his mark in 1988 with California spa food at the Sonoma Mission Inn and now offers his own style of cooking at his Eastside Oyster Bar and Grill. Chef and restaurateur John Ash has used Asian cooking techniques and ingredients in basic American fare in his restaurant in Santa Rosa and in the kitchen and cooking school at Fetzer Vineyard in Hopland. Todd Muir, with his exciting, experimental palate, is yet another innovator. Since he opened the Madrona Manor restaurant in 1983, we have been treated to a classic Italian cuisine enlivened with Hispanic and Northern Californian touches.

Further afield, in Mendocino, with its dense redwood forests and the constant presence of the ocean, the food matches the spirit of wildness, simplicity, and escape. One of the pioneers who shaped north-coast cuisine was Margaret Fox, who established her no-nonsense cooking style at the Mendocino Hotel in 1975. In 1977, she moved over a few streets to the existing Cafe Beaujolais, where her simple-is-better formula put Mendocino dining on the map. Rosemary Campiformio sets her own style at St. Orres, in tiny Gualala. The restaurant may look like something in a Russian fairy tale, but Rosemary's food is all California—

redolent with fresh herbs from the kitchen garden and sparked with a quirky sense of experimentation.

When I think back to the sweet picnic days of the fifties, I realize just how extraordinary the wine country is today. Daily, some of our country's finest chefs awaken to hear the sound of birdsong instead of traffic, and they serve foods grown minutes from their kitchens rather than trucked in from a distance. It is an exciting time for growers, chefs, and diners alike. As today's chefs travel and work in kitchens around the world, new influences will continue to enrich the local cuisine.

I hope that you will find some favorite recipes and that preparing them will carry you back to our vine-covered valleys and hillsides. The wine country's pleasures are contagious. If you pulled up a chair next to any of the chefs in this book and asked why he or she chooses to live and cook in the wine country, I know, somehow, each one would reply, "For me, this is life as it is meant to be."

Antonia Allegra

Napa County

Bistro Don Giovanni

"What goes together better than wine and food?"
asks Donna Scala, the chef and co-owner of Bistro Don
Giovanni, which is on the St. Helena Highway (Highway
29) at the southern end of the Napa Valley. She and her
husband, Giovanni, well-known in the valley for being
the original owners and chefs of the Piatti restaurant
chain, draw their inspiration from the valley's fine wines,
physical beauty, and abundant harvests.

"The valley is so tranquil, it brings out your most creative
energies," Scala says. "The smells at harvest time, the mustard in bloom, the farmers' market—it truly is a paradise
on earth." In the bistro's butter yellow dining room, with
its exposed kitchen and wraparound porch, and in the
warm atmosphere that fills it, diners can sense the tranquil-
lity. "People should feel comforted while dining," she
explains, "like guests in a friend's home."

Bistro Don Giovanni offers authentic Italian cuisine that
welcomes French and American influences. Along with
traditional grilled sausages, robust risotto, and capellini
with tomato, basil, and garlic, there are a bistro burger
with French fries, a salmon fillet with mashed potatoes,
and an aged New York steak with onion rings.

"My approach to food is straightforward and unpretentious," Scala says. "It makes you feel comforted, yet very
special; clean flavors that make you want more. Fresh
ingredients are the most important part of my food." The
bistro takes its name from Donna's and Giovanni's first
names. "It was good enough for Mozart," she says with
a twinkle in her eye, "so why not?"

COMICE PEAR AND STILTON SALAD

Serves 4. Wine recommendation: a dry, crisp Sauvignon Blanc

Candied Walnuts

2/3 cup peanut or canola oil
16 walnut halves
1 tablespoon confectioners' sugar
Pinch of salt

Sherry and Walnut Vinaigrette

1 1/2 tablespoons sherry vinegar
2 tablespoons chopped shallots
3 tablespoons walnut oil
1 1/2 tablespoons olive oil
Salt and pepper, to taste

3 Comice pears
2 bunches *frisée*, cut into bite-sized pieces
1 head radicchio, julienned
Salt and pepper, to taste
8 ounces Stilton cheese, crumbled

Candied Walnuts

Heat the oil in a small saucepan over medium-high heat. While the oil is heating, drop the walnuts into boiling water and boil for 10 seconds. Remove the nuts with a slotted spoon and toss them in a bowl with the sugar and salt. Immediately transfer the walnuts to the hot oil and stir them until the sugar caramelizes.

Using a dry slotted spoon, remove the candied walnuts and let them cool in a single layer on a baking sheet.

Sherry and Walnut Vinaigrette

Combine the vinegar and shallots in a small bowl. Whisk in the oils and season with salt and pepper. *Makes 1/3 cup.*

To assemble the salad, quarter and core the pears and gently warm them in a sauté pan over low heat with a small quantity of the vinaigrette. (Alternatively, prepare a charcoal grill, brush the pears lightly with olive oil, and cook approximately 1 to 2 minutes on each side.) Place the *frisée* and radicchio in a bowl, season with salt and pepper and toss with the remaining vinaigrette. Divide the lettuce mixture among 4 plates and place the warm pears on top. Garnish with the Stilton and the cooled walnuts. Serve immediately.

1 pound (2 1/2 cups) large white beans

1/4 cup olive oil

4 whole lamb shanks (approximately
    4 pounds)

6 cups chicken stock or low-sodium
    canned chicken broth

8 cloves garlic, peeled and crushed

1 stalk celery, roughly chopped
    (approximately 1 cup)

1 small carrot, roughly chopped

Salt and pepper, to taste

1 yellow onion, peeled and chopped
    (approximately 1 cup)

1 tablespoon rosemary, roughly chopped

1 cup diced tomatoes

1/4 cup roughly chopped flat-leaf
    Italian parsley

1/4 cup roughly chopped fresh thyme

Zest of 1 lemon

Zest of 1 orange

BRAISED LAMB SHANKS WITH WHITE BEANS

Serves 4. Wine recommendation: a full-bodied Cabernet Sauvignon with a hint of smoke

A Note on Procedure

Soak the beans in cold water for at least 3 hours before you start the lamb.

Preheat the oven to 300 degrees F, unless you plan to braise the lamb shanks on top of the stove.

While the beans are soaking, heat a roasting pan large enough to hold the shanks in 1 layer over medium heat on the stove top. Add the oil and raise the heat. Brown the shanks thoroughly, approximately 5 minutes on each side. Do not salt. Add the chicken stock, half of the garlic, the celery and the carrot. Bring the mixture to a simmer. Cover and let the shanks braise at the barest simmer, either on top of the stove or in the oven, until they are very tender, approximately 1 to 1 1/2 hours. Turn the shanks at least once. When the lamb is nearly cooked, season with the salt and pepper.

When the beans have finished soaking, drain them and discard the soaking water. Place the beans, onion, remaining garlic and the rosemary in a 4-quart saucepan. Cover with cold water and simmer until the beans are tender, approximately 1 to 1 1/2 hours. Check that water is always covering the beans, replenishing if necessary, and stir frequently but gently.

When the beans are cooked, remove them from the heat and stir in the tomatoes, parsley and thyme. Season with salt and pepper. To serve, ladle a generous cup of the beans into the center of 4 warm plates and place a shank on top. Garnish with the lemon and orange zests. (This entire dish may be prepared ahead of time and reheated.)

CHOCOLATE-POLENTA MOUSSE CAKE

Makes one 8-inch cake. Wine recommendation: a late-harvest Riesling

Chocolate Mousse

1 cup heavy cream

8 ounces semisweet chocolate, chopped

1/2 teaspoon vanilla extract

Pinch of salt

3 extra-large egg whites

1 tablespoon sugar

Chocolate-Polenta Cake

7 large eggs, separated

1 tablespoon sugar

6 ounces semisweet chocolate

6 tablespoons unsalted butter

1 tablespoon vanilla extract

1/4 cup polenta

Pinch of salt

3 tablespoons rum

Whipped cream (or ice cream) and chocolate shavings, for garnish

Chocolate Mousse

Heat the cream in a small saucepan until it is very hot. Place the chocolate in a mixing bowl and pour the cream over it. Stir frequently until the mixture is cool. Stir in the vanilla and salt. In a separate bowl, beat the egg whites until they are frothy, slowly add the sugar and whip until soft peaks form. Fold the egg whites into the chocolate mixture. Refrigerate for 2 hours.

Chocolate-Polenta Cake

While the mousse is chilling, prepare the cake. Preheat the oven to 350 degrees F. Line with parchment paper, grease and flour an 8-inch cake pan.

In a bowl, whisk the egg whites until they are frothy. Slowly add the sugar and whisk until soft peaks form. In a double boiler, melt the chocolate and butter. Remove from the heat and let cool slightly. With an electric mixer, beat the egg yolks on low speed until they are pale in color; add the chocolate mixture, vanilla, polenta, salt and rum. Fold the egg whites into the yolk mixture. Pour the batter into the pan and bake the cake for 20 to 25 minutes, or until a skewer inserted into the middle comes out clean. Let the cake cool for 10 minutes in the pan and then remove it. Refrigerate the cake for 1 hour to make splitting it easier.

To serve, split the cake in half horizontally with a serrated knife and spread the mousse between the 2 layers. (Because the cake is dense and very thin, it might be difficult to split horizontally. The cake may also be cut in half to make 2 half-moons, the mousse spread on one half, then the second half placed on top.) Refrigerate the cake for 30 minutes. Cut the cake into 4 pieces and serve with whipped cream and chocolate shavings.

Domaine Chandon Restaurant

The list of chefs with whom Philippe Jeanty trained reads like a Who's Who of French haute cuisine: Gaston Lenôtre, Gérard Boyer, Jean-Pierre Lallement, and the Troisgros brothers. Yet Jeanty, the chef at Domaine Chandon, says that his style of cooking comes from earlier experience which predates his training.

"I used to climb up in the attic of our farmhouse to smell the pears and apples stored on the wooden planks," he says of his youth in the Champagne region of France. "We used to pick wild thyme and rosemary in the hills, and I remember learning there that lavender flowers add a wonderful perfume to crème brûlée." These early adventures with foods inspire Jeanty's cooking today. "The cuisine doesn't have true content, or heart," he says, "unless you have the emotional memories to work with."

Like Jeanty, the restaurant at Domaine Chandon has its roots in the Champagne region, where Moët-Hennessy, the parent company of Domaine Chandon, operates well-known restaurants in the French wine country. Jeanty's family have worked for Moët as grape growers and wine makers for two generations, and Jeanty was a chef for Moët before coming to California.

The grandeur and refinement of the winery and visitors' center contrast with the earthy, essential aromas that emanate from the kitchen. Jeanty favors bold tastes and textures such as those of wild mushrooms, French truffles, smoked red trout, and local cheeses and game, and pairs them with Domaine Chandon's méthode champenoise sparkling wines for an epicurean experience reminiscent of his native country.

SMOKED RED TROUT MARINATED IN OLIVE OIL

Serves 8. Wine recommendation: a dry Chenin Blanc

A Note on Procedure

If you plan on smoking the trout, you will need to start 4 days ahead.

4 fillets red-meat trout (each weighing approximately 8 ounces), with the skin left on, or 8 slices (2 ounces each) freshly smoked salmon*

4 tablespoons kosher salt

Hickory and alderwood smoking chips

3 cups virgin olive oil

8 bay leaves

1/2 cup whole black peppercorns

16 sprigs fresh thyme

Half a yellow onion, sliced paper thin

1 carrot, sliced paper thin

1 head *frisée*

8 small Yellow Finn or Yukon Gold potatoes, steamed or boiled in salted water

Cracked black pepper, for garnish

Chervil or parsley, for garnish

Balsamic vinegar, for drizzling

*If you are using smoked salmon, omit the salting and smoking procedures.

Place the trout, skin side down, on a baking sheet and sprinkle evenly with the salt, using as much as you would for a dense covering on a thick steak. Let the fish sit, uncovered, in the refrigerator for 2 days to cure.

In a smoker, cold-smoke the fillets for 6 to 8 hours, isolating the heat source by using one container for smoldering the wood chips and then venting the smoke to another that holds the trout. In this way, only the smoke, not the heat, will affect the trout. The smoke should be very light.

After the trout is smoked, let it rest for 1 day, uncovered, in the refrigerator. Then remove the skin and marinate the fillets overnight in the refrigerator, uncovered, in the olive oil with the bay leaves, peppercorns, thyme, onion and carrot. (If you are using smoked salmon, it should be marinated the same way.)

When you are ready to serve, strain the marinade off the fish, reserving the oil and the marinated vegetables separately. Arrange the *frisee* on plates with the carrot slices from the marinade. If necessary, reheat the potatoes until just warm, then slice and arrange them on the plates. Slice the trout fillets into 5 pieces or break in half, if you prefer, and arrange the fish over the potatoes. Drape the onion over the fish and garnish with the cracked pepper and chervil. Drizzle some of the marinade oil and the balsamic vinegar over the salad and serve.

SEA BASS WITH LENTILS AND MASHED POTATOES

Serves 6. Wine recommendation: an aged sparkling wine

Lentils
Lentils
1/2 pound (2 cups) green French lentils
1 quart plus 1 1/4 cups chicken stock
5 1/2 ounces applewood-smoked bacon;
   3 1/2 ounces of it in 3 large chunks,
   the rest sliced and julienned
1/2 tablespoon kosher salt, plus extra for
   seasoning
1 teaspoon freshly ground black pepper,
   plus extra for seasoning
2 small yellow onions
2 carrots
2 bay leaves
5 sprigs fresh thyme, plus 6 sprigs
   for garnish
Half a head garlic, cut horizontally,
   plus 1 teaspoon chopped garlic

Mashed Potatoes
3 large baking potatoes, peeled and cut
   into chunks
8 slices (8 ounces) applewood-smoked
   bacon
4 tablespoons unsalted butter
3/4 teaspoon salt
1/4 teaspoon freshly ground black pepper

2 teaspoons olive oil
5 tablespoons unsalted butter
4 tablespoons balsamic vinegar
6 fillets Chilean sea bass (5 ounces each)

Lentils
Combine the lentils with 1 quart of the stock, the 3 chunks of bacon, and the salt and pepper in a large saucepan. Cut one of the onions and one of the carrots into eighths and tie them, together with the bay leaves, 3 sprigs of the thyme and the half head of garlic, in a square of cheesecloth and add the bundle to the lentils. Cook over low heat for 25 to 30 minutes, or until the lentils are tender.

While the lentils are simmering, prepare the mashed potatoes.

Mashed Potatoes
Cook the potatoes in boiling salted water for 20 minutes. Cook the bacon slices in a skillet over medium-high heat until they are crisp and then dice them finely. Set the bacon aside. When the potatoes are soft, drain them and mash them with a potato masher or push them through a potato ricer; you should have 3 cups. Mix in the bacon, butter, salt and pepper and set aside, keeping warm.

To finish the lentils, dice the remaining onion and sauté it in a large saucepan over medium heat for 3 minutes in 1 teaspoon of the olive oil and 1 tablespoon of the butter, with 2 sprigs of thyme. Dice the remaining carrot and blanch the pieces by dropping them into boiling water for 2 minutes, then draining them and cooling them under cold running water; set the carrot aside.

Preheat the oven to 500 degrees F.

Strain the cooked lentils, discarding any liquid and the bacon chunks. Add the lentils to the sautéed onion, pour in 3/4 cup of the remaining chicken stock and bring the mixture to a boil. Lower the heat, add the julienned bacon and simmer for 5 minutes. Add the blanched carrot, 2 tablespoons of the vinegar, 1/4 cup stock, and salt and pepper. Simmer for another 5 minutes. Add the last 1/4 cup stock and the remaining 2 tablespoons vinegar; gently stir in the chopped garlic and 3 tablespoons of the butter. Keep the lentils warm while the fish is being cooked.

Season the fish with salt and pepper. In a nonstick, ovenproof pan, melt the remaining olive oil and butter. Brown the sea bass lightly over medium heat on the top of the stove. Transfer the pan to the oven and roast the fish for 8 to 10 minutes, turning once.

To serve, place a portion of lentils in a bowl, top with 2 generous spoonfuls of mashed potatoes and arrange the sea bass on the potatoes. Top with a sprig of thyme.

PEAR, BANANA AND CHOCOLATE SORBETS

Serves 6. Wine recommendation: a late-harvest Riesling or late-harvest Muscat

Pear Sorbet

Pear Sorbet

1 cup sugar

1 cup water

10 ripe, flavorful pears

1/4 cup lemon juice, or to taste

Mix the sugar and water in a saucepan, bring the mixture to a boil and set it aside to cool.

Run the pears through a Champion Juicer and place in a medium-sized bowl. Immediately add the lemon juice and the cooled syrup to the pear juice. Lacking a Champion Juicer, peel and core the pears and purée them in a food processor with the syrup and lemon juice. Strain the purée through a sieve.

Following the manufacturer's directions, pour the sorbet into an ice-cream machine and freeze it. *Makes 1 quart.*

Banana Sorbet

Banana Sorbet

12 ripe bananas, peeled and frozen for at least 4 hours or overnight

Chocolate sauce (optional)

Chill the attachment of a Champion Juicer in the freezer for 15 minutes (with "blank" screen on). At serving time, place the attachment on the juicer and run the frozen bananas through it. If you do not have a Champion Juicer, peel the bananas, cut them into 2-inch chunks and freeze them for 3 to 4 hours. Purée them in a food processor and serve at once. *Makes 1 quart.*

Chocolate Sorbet

Chocolate Sorbet

4 1/2 cups water

2 1/2 cups cocoa powder (preferably Valrhona)

2 1/4 cups plus 2 tablespoons granulated sugar

Whisk the water, cocoa and sugar together in a medium saucepan and bring the mixture to a boil. Remove the pan from the heat and set aside to cool. Following the manufacturer's directions, pour the mixture into an ice cream machine and freeze it. *Makes 1 1/2 quarts.*

Serve the trio of sorbets, together or by themselves, topping the banana sorbet with chocolate sauce, if desired.

Mustards Grill

You can eat your way from San Francisco to the Napa Valley without ever straying from the soul-satisfying food of celebrated chef Cindy Pawlcyn, whose restaurants include Bix, Bistro Rôti, and the Fog City Diner in San Francisco and the Buckeye Roadhouse north of the Golden Gate. But it all started at Mustards Grill in Napa, a down-home place known for its slabs of baby back ribs.

"Our concept from the beginning was to be a fun, lively restaurant serving big, soulful food," says Terry Lynch, the executive chef in charge of daily operations at Mustards. The fun begins with the dog paw prints on the walls, the rich scents emanating from the oak-burning grill, and the spirited conversations of the valley wine makers who frequent Mustards. The size and soulfulness of the food come from the meeting of Pawlcyn's vision, Lynch's talent and training, and the chefs' access to outstanding ingredients.

"With cooking as unembellished as ours, we have to start with exceptional products," Lynch says. "I spend a lot of energy building relationships with people who provide the finest, most flavorful fruits and vegetables. Local pickers keep us supplied with incredible mushrooms, and we have a long-standing rapport with local farmers who provide us with great lamb, goats, pigs, ducks, and chickens."

Lynch started in the restaurant business as a sommelier, then became hooked on the "vitality and intensity" he found in the kitchen. Today, he says that his wine-country cooking "boils down to great ingredients worked in a seemingly simple manner that has all the straightforward sparkle of a ride in the countryside."

GRILLED STUFFED PASILLA PEPPERS
WITH TOMATILLO SALSA

Serves 6. Wine recommendation: a slightly herbaceous, crisp Sauvignon Blanc, with citrus flavor

6 large *pasilla* chiles

Corn Stuffing

1 teaspoon unsalted butter

1 shallot, minced

1 clove garlic, minced

2 ears corn, grated on a hand grater (grating the kernels by hand preserves more flavor)

1 1/3 cups cream

Pinch of salt

Dash of Tabasco sauce

Pinch of nutmeg

Pinch of freshly ground white pepper

1/3 cup instant white corn grits

1/2 cup grated Cheddar cheese

Tomatillo Salsa

1/2 pound tomatillos

1 red Fresno chile

2 cups arugula

Half a red onion, chopped

1 bunch cilantro, chopped

Pinch of salt

Pinch of freshly ground black pepper

A few drops of Spanish sherry vinegar

Sprigs of cilantro, for garnish

Char the *pasillas* over an open flame until the skin is blistered and blackened. (Lacking an open flame, coat the chiles lightly with olive oil and blacken them in a preheated 450-degree-F oven, turning them frequently.) Cool slightly and peel them carefully. Cut a lengthwise slit in each chile and reach in with a small knife or your fingers and remove the seeds; it is now ready to be stuffed.

Corn Stuffing

Melt the butter in a saucepan, add the shallot and garlic and sauté them over medium-high heat for 1 minute without browning them. Add the corn and continue to sauté, stirring often. Add the cream, salt, Tabasco, nutmeg and pepper and continue to stir often. When the mixture begins to boil, stir in the grits and cook until thickened. This will take approximately 4 to 5 minutes and will require considerable stirring. Once the grits are cooked, remove the pan from the heat, stir in the cheese until it has just melted and pour the mixture into a bowl to cool.

Tomatillo Salsa

At the restaurant, the most popular salsa for these *pasillas* is definitely our tomatillo salsa. To prepare the salsa, peel off and discard the papery husks of the tomatillos, place them in a saucepan, add water to cover and bring the water to a quick boil. Drain the tomatillos in a colander and refresh them under cold running water (or in a bowl of ice water) until they are cool. Place the tomatillos in a blender with the chile, arugula, onion, cilantro, salt, pepper and vinegar and pulse to make a slightly chunky salsa. Taste for seasoning: It might need more vinegar to pump up the acidity. If you are not planning to serve the salsa immediately, set it aside, but do not refrigerate. If the salsa is too cold, it won't pop with flavor.

To stuff the chiles, carefully open the slit and spoon in some of the cooled stuffing. Roll the chile between your hands to push the stuffing toward the two ends. At this point, the chiles can be heated and served immediately or refrigerated for later use.

We like to heat them on our wood-burning grill: First we rub them with a teaspoon or so of olive oil, then grill them until they are hot in the center. Otherwise, place them in a preheated, 350-degree-F oven for 10 minutes or until they are heated through.

To serve, pour a little of the room-temperature tomatillo salsa on 6 plates, arrange the hot *pasillas* on top and garnish with the cilantro.

1 tablespoon brown sugar

1 1/2 tablespoons water

4 tablespoons Dijon mustard

2 tablespoons cider vinegar

1 teaspoon salt

1/2 teaspoon freshly ground white pepper

1/2 teaspoon chopped thyme

1/2 teaspoon Worcestershire sauce

2 cloves garlic, chopped

6 portions skirt steak (6 ounces each),
  trimmed of excess fat and sinew

Pepper Catsup

1 tablespoon olive oil

1/4 cup diced red onion

5 green onions, diced

Half a red bell pepper, diced

Half a yellow bell pepper, diced

3 red Fresno chiles, finely diced

2 whole *chipotle* chiles in *adobo* sauce,
  diced

1 clove garlic, minced

Pinch of thyme

1/2 teaspoon salt

Pinch of cayenne pepper

1/2 cup commercial catsup

1/2 teaspoon freshly ground white pepper

GRILLED SKIRT STEAK WITH PEPPER CATSUP

Serves 6. Wine recommendation: a fruity, forward-style Zinfandel

Marinade

In a medium-sized bowl, combine the sugar, water, mustard, vinegar, salt, pepper, thyme, Worcestershire sauce and garlic. Take each piece of skirt steak and rub the marinade into it with your hands. Place the steaks in a nonreactive bowl and refrigerate, covered, for at least 6 hours.

Pepper Catsup

Heat the oil in a saucepan. Add the onions, bell peppers, chiles, garlic, thyme, salt and cayenne and cook the mixture over medium heat, covered, for 5 minutes. Add the catsup and white pepper and cook for 5 minutes more or until thick.

Just before serving, prepare a charcoal fire grill or heat an electric grill to high. Grill the steaks for 1 1/2 minutes on each side. Serve with pepper catsup.

JACK DANIELS CHOCOLATE CAKE

Makes one 10-inch cake; serves 6 to 8. Wine recommendation: a late-harvest Zinfandel or a vintage character Port

2 tablespoons unsalted butter

6 ounces chocolate

Pinch of salt

8 eggs, separated

3/4 cup plus 2 tablespoons sugar

2 cups ground pecans

2 tablespoons Jack Daniels whiskey

Pinch of cream of tartar

Chocolate sauce, butterscotch sauce and whipped cream, for garnish (optional)

Butter and flour a 10-inch cake pan and preheat the oven to 375 degrees F.

Place the butter, chocolate and salt in a metal bowl over simmering water and stir occasionally until the mixture is smooth.

Beat the egg yolks and the 3/4 cup sugar in a mixing bowl until the mixture is a pale gold and falls in folds from the beaters. Stir in the chocolate mixture, the pecans and the whiskey.

In a separate bowl, beat the egg whites with the cream of tartar until soft peaks form; then add the 2 tablespoons sugar and beat until stiff but not dry. Stir one-fourth of the egg white mixture into the chocolate mixture to lighten the batter, then fold in the rest of the egg white mixture until the batter is smooth. Pour the batter into the cake pan and bake until a skewer inserted in the center comes out clean, approximately 45 to 55 minutes. Set the cake aside to cool in the pan.

Once cool, unmold the cake, slice it and serve it with chocolate sauce, butterscotch sauce and whipped cream, if desired.

Stars Oakville Cafe

Fans of Jeremiah Tower's eateries, such as Stars in San Francisco, can now sample a more rustic version of his cooking in the Napa Valley, at the Stars Oakville Cafe. Tower opened the cafe in October 1993, next door to the famed Oakville Grocery, and it has been a popular stop for wine tasters ever since.

Tower is often referred to as the "father of California cuisine." At Stars Oakville Cafe, though, you can forget trends and competitions and dig into hearty food whose fresh flavors stand up to the sturdiest Napa wines.

Beef, chicken, and lamb are roasted in a wood-burning oven that was custom-built for the cafe. House-made sausages are grilled over a flame, and artichoke hearts are baked with freshly picked marjoram and goat cheese produced by Laura Chenel, a cheese maker based in Sonoma County. On a recent lunch menu, every entree except the Nieman-Schell hamburger included roasted vegetables or roasted potatoes—or both.

The Cafe is actually a fair-sized restaurant, with seating for 100 evenly divided between the dining room and a garden patio. Inside, tile floors and bare walls accentuate the friendly rattle of crockery and the lively buzz of conversation. Big plate-glass windows give diners a view into the surprisingly small kitchen. The patio has awnings in summer and space heaters for cool evenings in the spring and fall.

PUMPKIN-FILLED PASTA GRATIN WITH ROAST FENNEL

Serves 4. Wine recommendation: a floral Sauvignon Blanc with melon and citrus flavors

Pumpkin Filling

Pumpkin Filling
1 small pumpkin (approximately 4 pounds)
   or 1 cup canned pumpkin
1 egg
3 tablespoons finely grated Parmesan cheese
1/4 teaspoon ground cinnamon
1/4 teaspoon ground nutmeg
1/4 teaspoon ground cloves
1 1/2 teaspoons finely chopped fresh sage
1/2 cup fine dry bread crumbs
Salt and freshly ground black pepper,
   to taste

Gratin
1/2 pound fresh pasta sheets, cut
   into 8 rectangles, each measuring
   3 1/2 by 4 1/2 inches
1 cup grated Parmesan cheese
1 cup heavy cream
2 teaspoons finely chopped sage
2 teaspoons finely chopped thyme
1/4 cup grated fontina cheese

3 cups fennel, julienned
3 tablespoons olive oil
Salt and freshly ground black pepper,
   to taste
White truffle oil (optional)

Pumpkin Filling

Preheat the oven to 350 degrees F.

Cut the pumpkin into quarters and clean out the seeds. In a roasting pan lined with aluminum foil, lay the pumpkin, skin side down, on a wire rack and cover the pan lightly with aluminum foil. Bake for one hour or until the pumpkin is tender; remove, let cool. Leave the oven on.

Scoop 1 cup of the pumpkin flesh into a bowl, being careful not to scoop in bits of rind. (Reserve any remaining pumpkin for another use.) Add the egg and mix, then add the Parmesan, spices and sage. Fold in the bread crumbs in increments until the filling is dry and firm; if it is too wet, add more bread crumbs. Season with salt and pepper.

Gratin

Drop the pasta pieces one by one into a large pot of salted, boiling water, being careful they do not overlap. Cook to just past the al dente stage. Remove the pieces carefully and dip them in a bowl of cold water (do not rinse under running water).

Drain the pasta well and lay out each piece on a work surface sprinkled with approximately one third of the Parmesan, then sprinkle the pasta with another third of the Parmesan. At the bottom of each rectangle of pasta place a golf ball–sized dollop of pumpkin filling and carefully and lightly roll up the pasta to enclose the filling. Lift the pasta carefully and make sure that it has been rolled up evenly. Holding the pasta roll lightly between the fingertips, push the filling in toward the middle of the roll from both sides to square it up and fold the ends over. You should have a small brick of pumpkin-filled pasta, approximately 2 inches long and 1 1/2 inches wide, with the ends neatly folded as if it were a small parcel.

Butter an 8-inch-square ovenproof gratin dish and place the pasta packages into the dish, arranged in 2 rows of 4 across. Pour the cream over the pasta. Sprinkle the sage, thyme and fontina over each piece and then sprinkle on the remaining Parmesan. Bake the gratin for 20 to 30 minutes, or until the cheese is golden and the cream is bubbling.

Meanwhile, toss the fennel with the olive oil and salt and pepper and place it in a small ovenproof pan and bake it for 20 minutes, or until it is tender.

To serve, put the warm fennel on the plate, then spoon on 2 pieces of pasta with some of the cream. A light drizzle of white truffle oil, if using, beautifully highlights the pasta.

RED WINE–BRAISED BEEF CHEEKS WITH ROOT VEGETABLE PURÉE AND BRAISED RED ONIONS

Serves 4. Wine recommendation: a big, bold Cabernet Sauvignon

4 beef cheeks, cleaned of fat and silverskin,
   or 4 portions (6 ounces each)
   chuck roast
Salt and freshly ground black pepper
12 cloves garlic, unpeeled
6 bay leaves
6 sprigs fresh thyme
1/2 teaspoon chopped fresh rosemary
1 (750 ml) bottle good red wine
1 quart veal stock (or rich meat stock)

Root Vegetable Purée
4 carrots, peeled and cut into 1-inch dice
4 turnips, peeled and cut into 1-inch dice
4 celery roots, peeled and cut into
   1-inch dice
4 tablespoons unsalted butter

6 large red onions, peeled and sliced thinly
1/4 cup olive oil

Preheat the oven to 300 degrees F.

Season the beef generously with salt and pepper and put it into a dry casserole or heavy pot with the garlic, bay leaves, thyme and rosemary. On the stove top, brown the beef over medium heat for 15 minutes, turning it every 3 minutes. Cover with the red wine and stock and cook in the oven until the meat is tender, approximately 2 1/2 hours.

Root Vegetable Purée

While the beef is cooking, boil the carrots, turnips and celery roots in a large pot of salted water until tender, approximately 10 to 20 minutes. (You may want to start the celery root first because it takes longer to cook.) Mash the vegetables with the butter and season with salt and pepper to taste.

Place the onions and the olive oil in a small, heavy-bottomed pan, add salt and pepper and cook, covered, over medium-low heat until they are soft, between 20 and 30 minutes.

Once the beef is cooked, remove it from the pot, cover and set it aside in a warm place. Strain the cooking liquid and press the garlic through the sieve. Return the liquid to the pot, and reduce the liquid over high heat by half, taking care to skim any fat from the top.

To serve, place a portion of the root vegetable purée on a plate and top with the beef. Pour the sauce over the beef and garnish with the red onions.

BAKED APPLE CARAMEL WITH BERRY SAUCE

1 1/2 cups sugar

1 cup water

4 apples (preferably pippin, McIntosh
   or Black Jonathan)

1 vanilla bean, split lengthwise

2 teaspoons grated lemon zest

1/4 teaspoon salt

1/2 cup unsalted butter, softened

1 tablespoon flour

3 eggs, beaten

Berry Sauce

1 cup raspberries or strawberries

1 tablespoon sugar, or to taste

Lemon juice, to taste

Crème fraîche, for garnish

Serves 4. Wine recommendation: a late-harvest Riesling

Preheat the oven to 350 degrees F.

To make the caramel, put 1 cup of the sugar and the water into a small pan and stir to combine. Cook over medium heat until the caramel is a rich, golden brown. Very carefully pour a small amount of caramel into each of four 5-ounce ramekins and rotate them so that the caramel covers the bottom and sides. Pour any excess back into the pan. Set the ramekins aside.

Peel, core and cut the apples into 1/8-inch-thick slices. Cook them slowly over low heat in a medium pan with the vanilla bean, zest, remaining 1/2 cup sugar and salt until the apples can be easily mashed with a spoon. If the apples are browning, cover the pan with a lid for a few minutes. Put the apple mixture into a bowl and let cool slightly. Scrape the vanilla bean and discard the pod. Mix in the butter, then the flour and last, the beaten eggs.

Divide the apple mixture evenly among the 4 ramekins, pressing it down lightly. Put the ramekins in a pan containing enough warm water to reach halfway up the sides of the ramekins and bake for 30 to 35 minutes, or until the mixture is set and a knife comes out clean. Serve immediately or let the ramekins sit at room temperature until you are ready to serve. Then reheat them at 350 degrees F for 5 to 10 minutes, until the caramel has liquefied and the dessert is warm in the center—test with a knife.

Berry Sauce
Purée the berries with the sugar and lemon juice and pass the mixture through a fine sieve to strain out the seeds.

To serve, unmold the apple caramel onto a plate and garnish with a dollop of *crème fraîche* and 2 tablespoons of berry sauce.

Auberge du Soleil

The southwestern ambiance of the Auberge du Soleil, conveyed in the cedar columns, peach-stuccoed walls, timbered ceilings, and fireplace contrasts with the European feel of its French doors, table linens, and floral bouquets. Step out onto the terrace and there's no question about where you are: Perched above the Silverado Trail, overlooking the Napa Valley's terraced vineyard floor, and gazing across toward the Mayacamas Mountains in the west.

Auberge du Soleil ("The Inn of the Sun") is among the region's most celebrated resorts, and its restaurant is one of its chief attractions. The kitchen has been under the direction of David Hale as executive chef since 1992. Hale's training in New England, including a stint at the famed Le Languedoc on Nantucket, is an excellent foil for the sun-splashed warmth of wine-country cuisine.

You'll often find lobster on the menu, for example, but it may be a lobster sausage stuffed with fresh, locally grown herbs such as fennel and mustard. Hale will also pair wild mallard duck with grilled butternut squash, and smoke fresh salmon over grapevine coals. "We change the menu constantly so we can focus on products that may be at their peak for only a short time," Hale says. "Going to work takes on added meaning when I stop to pick up the beautiful products from local farmers."

At Auberge, as the locals refer to it, deciding what to eat is preceded by deciding where to eat it. The expanded bar menu now offers a dozen dishes and a score of fine wines by the glass. If the weather's fine, though, you may want to take your meal outside onto the terrace and feel the warmth of the sun that gave Auberge du Soleil its name.

GOAT CHEESE TARTLETS

5 ounces *mascarpone*

5 ounces *chèvre* (a creamy, fresh
   goat cheese)

2 ounces soft, aged goat cheese

1 egg

2 tablespoons chopped fresh marjoram

6 sheets phyllo dough

6 tablespoons unsalted butter, melted

Poached Garlic

1 cup olive oil

18 large garlic cloves, peeled

Garlic Balsamic Vinaigrette

2 shallots, minced

1/2 cup balsamic vinegar

3/4 cup garlic oil (from the poached garlic)

1 tablespoon chopped marjoram

1/2 teaspoon salt

1 teaspoon cracked black pepper

6 cups mixed baby greens

2 tomatoes, seeded and diced

Serves 6. Wine recommendation: a barrel-fermented Sauvignon Blanc

Preheat the oven to 400 degrees F.

   In a mixer combine the *mascarpone, chèvre,* aged goat cheese, egg and marjoram. Using the paddles, blend the mixture until smooth.

   Brush each sheet of phyllo with 1 tablespoon of the melted butter, fold it into quarters and press it gently into the muffin cup of a standard muffin pan.

   Fill each cup three-quarters full with the cheese mixture and bake the tartlets in the oven for 20 minutes, or until golden brown.

Poached Garlic

In a medium sauté pan, combine the olive oil and garlic and simmer until the garlic is tender and golden, approximately 10 to 12 minutes.

   Remove the pan from the heat and allow the garlic to cool in the oil. Drain and reserve both the garlic and the oil.

Garlic Balsamic Vinaigrette

Whisk all the ingredients together. *Makes 1 1/4 cups.*

To serve, toss the greens and tomatoes with enough garlic balsamic vinaigrette to coat them and place a small quantity on each of six plates. Place a tartlet on one side of greens and garnish the plate with the poached garlic cloves. Drizzle the remaining vinaigrette over the garlic.

AHI AND SALMON TEMPURA SUSHI

Serves 6. Wine recommendation: a crisp Viognier

Tempura Batter
1 cup plus 1 tablespoon flour
1/3 cup cornstarch
2 egg yolks
1 1/4 cups ice water
Pinch of salt

1/4 pound *shiitake* mushrooms, stemmed
and sliced thinly
1 tablespoon sesame oil
1 teaspoon rice vinegar
6 ounces *sushi*-quality ahi tuna, in 1 piece
6 ounces salmon fillet, in 1 piece
1 teaspoon *wasabi* paste
1 teaspoon Japanese *sushi* spice*
2 sheets *nori** (sheets of dried seaweed)
3 cups peanut or canola oil

Pickled Ginger Vinaigrette
2 teaspoons sesame seeds
2 green onions, sliced very thinly
2 teaspoons grated fresh ginger
2 small cloves garlic, minced
1 tablespoon chopped cilantro
1 tablespoon chopped pickled ginger*
1/2 cup soy sauce
2 tablespoons pickled ginger juice
(from a jar of pickled ginger)
1 1/2 teaspoons sesame oil
1/2 teaspoon lemon juice

Shiso leaves, for garnish*
Daikon sprouts, for garnish
Enoki mushrooms, for garnish
Black sesame seeds, for garnish

*Available in Japanese markets.

Tempura Batter

Combine the flour and the cornstarch in a mixing bowl. Make a well in the center. Place the egg yolks and half of the water in the well and mix, using a wire whisk. Add the rest of the water to thin the paste to a light batter. Do not overwork; mix only until it is smooth. Season with salt.

The batter may be made up to 1 hour ahead of time, but must be kept very cold and stirred again before being used.

Sauté the mushrooms in the sesame oil. Just before they are done cooking, add the rice vinegar. Set aside to cool.

Cut the tuna and the salmon into 4 strips each measuring 1/2 inch by 1/2 inch by 3 inches. Spread one side of each strip with a thin layer of *wasabi* and sprinkle with *sushi* spice. Layer 3 or 4 slices of mushroom over the *wasabi* on each piece of tuna and place a piece of salmon, *wasabi*-side down, on top, creating a "sandwich." (The sandwiches may be made ahead of time and kept in the refrigerator.)

Roll 2 sandwiches in each sheet of *nori*, sealing the seam with water, and cut each roll into 3 equal pieces; this gives you 6 rolls.

In a deep saucepan preheat the oil to 375 degrees F. Dip each roll into the chilled batter, allowing the excess to drain back into the batter bowl, and carefully fry the rolls until the coating is crisp, but still pale. Do not cook until the crust is golden or the fish will be overcooked. Set the fried rolls aside.

Pickled Ginger Vinaigrette

Toast the sesame seeds in a preheated, dry skillet for approximately 3 minutes, tossing them and watching them closely because they burn easily. Set them aside to cool.

In a mixing bowl combine the green onions, fresh ginger, garlic, cilantro, pickled ginger, soy sauce, pickled ginger juice, sesame oil, lemon juice and toasted sesame seeds. Stir and taste the vinaigrette; no salt should be necessary. This dressing may be made up to 4 hours in advance. *Makes 2 cups.*

To serve, drizzle some of the pickled ginger vinaigrette over each plate, cut each fried roll in half to expose the colors of the fish, place on top the vinaigrette and garnish the plates with the *shiso* leaves, *daikon* sprouts and *enoki* mushrooms. Scatter the black sesame seeds on top and serve at once.

1 cup espresso or strong coffee

2 tablespoons plus 1/3 cup sugar

3 whole eggs

3 egg yolks

1 1/2 cups half-and-half

4 cups day-old croissant or brioche,
    cut into 1/2-inch cubes

1/2 cup sliced almonds (optional)

Caramel Sauce

1/2 cup sugar

1/4 cup water

3/4 cup heavy cream

2 tablespoons unsalted butter

Whipped cream, for garnish

Ground cinnamon, for garnish

WARM CAPPUCCINO BREAD PUDDING WITH CARAMEL SAUCE

Makes one 9-by-9-inch pudding; serves 6. Wine recommendation: a tawny Port

Combine the espresso and the 2 tablespoons sugar in a small saucepan over medium heat; stir until the sugar is dissolved. Reduce the mixture to 1/2 cup and set it aside to cool.

Combine the eggs, yolks and remaining 1/3 cup sugar in a medium mixing bowl and slowly stir in the half-and-half. Add the cooled espresso mixture and stir until all the ingredients are well mixed.

Preheat the oven to 325 degrees F.

Spread the croissant cubes evenly in a 9-by-9-by-2-inch baking pan or casserole dish. (At the restaurant, we bake and serve the pudding in oversized, ovenproof coffee cups.) Sprinkle the almonds evenly over the cubes.

Pour the liquid mixture into the pan, making sure that all the bread is submerged. Allow the bread to absorb all the liquid; this will take approximately 30 minutes. Place the baking pan into a water bath (a large pan containing enough water to fill it to a depth of 1/2 inch). Bake the pudding for approximately 1 hour, until it is golden brown and firm to the touch in the center.

Allow the pudding to sit briefly (approximately 10 minutes) before serving.

Caramel Sauce

Combine the sugar and water in a small saucepan and bring the mixture to a boil over medium heat. Occasionally brush down the sides of the pot with a pastry brush dipped in cold water to prevent crystals from forming. Cook the mixture until it turns a deep caramel color, registering approximately 325 degrees F on a candy thermometer. Remove the pan from the heat.

Slowly whisk in the heavy cream. *Caution: Adding cold cream to hot liquid will generate steam; be sure to stand back.* Stir in the butter until it has melted and set the mixture aside to rest for 10 minutes. *Makes 1 cup.*

Serve the pudding warm, topped with caramel sauce and whipped cream sprinkled with ground cinnamon.

The Restaurant at Meadowood

At dusk, diners at the Meadowood resort can watch deer grazing on the golf course and late summer shadows fall across the croquet lawn. Meanwhile, in the kitchen, executive chef Roy Breiman is creating a meal that unites the best of the California wine country with the flavors of a region thousands of miles away.

"My creative vision is to give our diners an experience close to what they would find in Provence," Breiman says. He recently returned to California after spending two years steeped in the flavors and cooking techniques of Michelin-starred restaurants in southern France, and has begun using ingredients available in and around St. Helena in the Provençal style he loves.

"My menus are inspired by the availability of products from season to season," he explains. "I like to emphasize the colors of spring, the bounty of summer, the transition of autumn, and the spices of winter." Once inspired, Breiman lets the seasonal flavors guide his preparation and presentation. "My food is simple but elegant, rustic yet refined," he says. "Mine is a sort of down-to-earth style using first-class and sophisticated products such as foie gras and truffles."

The Restaurant at Meadowood presents diners with a formidable challenge, but it's one they will almost certainly enjoy: choosing wine to complement the food. The wine list offers a vintage from every wine producer in the Napa Valley—a number that now exceeds 225.

WARM CALAMARI WITH WHITE BEAN VINAIGRETTE

Serves 4. Wine recommendation: a full-bodied Chardonnay with fairly solid oak

7 ounces (1 cup) Great Northern beans

1 yellow onion, sliced

3 slices bacon, cut into 1-inch pieces

Half a bunch fresh thyme

2 bay leaves

2 cups water mixed with 1 teaspoon salt

12 fresh whole calamari

3 shallots, chopped

2 bunches chives, chopped

3 tomatoes, diced

1/4 cup balsamic vinegar

1/4 cup olive oil

Salt and freshly ground white pepper,
   to taste

6 cloves garlic, finely chopped

12 sprigs flat-leaf Italian parsley

A Note on Procedure

Soak the beans in unsalted water for 3 or 4 hours before cooking. Drain and set them aside.

In a large pot, combine the onion, bacon, thyme and bay leaves. Brown this mixture lightly over medium-high heat before adding the drained beans and the 2 cups salted water. Cook over medium heat, covered, until the beans are tender, approximately 2 to 2 1/2 hours.

Clean the calamari by cutting off the tentacles and setting them aside, then removing the eye, the main cartilage and the rest of the insides. Rinse well and cut the calamari into 1/4-inch rings. Place the rings in a bowl with the tentacles and refrigerate until they are to be cooked.

Drain the cooked beans, reserving the cooking water, and place them with a little of the cooking water in a sauté pan. Combine the shallots, half of the chives, half of the tomato, the vinegar and 2 tablespoons of the olive oil and warm the mixture over medium heat. Season with salt and pepper and set the mixture aside.

In another sauté pan, combine the calamari with the remaining olive oil, tomato and chives and all of the garlic and cook over high heat for approximately 1 minute. Remove from the heat. Season to taste with salt and pepper.

To serve, spoon 6 or 7 large tablespoonfuls of the bean mixture onto each plate. Place a portion of calamari on top of the beans. Serve warm, garnished with Italian parsley.

MEDALLIONS OF LAMB WRAPPED IN RED ONION

Serves 4. Wine recommendation: a fairly intense Merlot

A Note on Procedure

Begin the lamb stock at least one day ahead.

Lamb Stock

Preheat the oven to 500 degrees F and roast the lamb bones in a roasting pan until they are dark brown. Remove the bones from the oven and drain off the fat. Place the bones, water, chicken stock, garlic, thyme and bay leaves into a large pot and cook over low heat for 4 hours, adding water whenever needed. Strain the mixture and refrigerate. The fat will solidify and should be removed and discarded.

Place the tenderloins between sheets of plastic wrap and flatten them until they are approximately 1/4 inch thick. Refrigerate the meat while preparing the vegetables.

Peel and cut the potato lengthwise into pieces 2 inches long and 1 inch wide. Set them aside in a bowl of cold water. Blanch the tomatoes in rapidly boiling water for 10 seconds. Peel them, cut them into quarters and remove the seeds. Cut the onions in half horizontally. Separate the outer two-thirds of each half into individual layers and set them aside; reserve the centers. In a small pot, cook the outer layers of the onions in salted boiling water with the vinegar until they are tender, approximately 15 to 20 minutes. Peel the zucchini carefully, slice the peel thinly and discard the remainder or reserve it for another use.

Place one of the lamb tenderloins on a flat surface. On top of the meat arrange three tomato quarters down the center and top them with some of the julienned zucchini peel. Season with salt and pepper. Roll the lamb to its original shape and place it on a leaf of pastry. Roll the tenderloin up in the pastry as you would an egg roll and seal the edges with some of the egg wash. Repeat the procedure with the second tenderloin. Cover and refrigerate the rolls.

To make the garnish, thinly slice the reserved onion centers. Heat a little of the olive oil in a sauté pan, add the potatoes, the onion slices and oregano. Cook over medium heat until the vegetables are brown. Add the lamb stock to pan; continue cooking gently for 5 minutes. Just before serving, add the remaining tomato quarters, the basil leaves and the outer layers of onion, and cook the mixture for 1 to 2 minutes until all the flavors are blended.

Season the loins with salt and pepper and cook them in a sauté pan in olive oil over medium-high heat until they are medium rare, approximately 8 minutes. Cook the pastry-wrapped tenderloins in a sauté pan in olive oil over medium heat until they are golden brown all over, approximately 3 minutes.

To serve, slice each lamb loin into 6 medallions, placing 3 on each plate. Arrange the garnish in layers on the medallions: 1 piece of potato, 1 tomato quarter, 1 basil leaf and, on top, 1 piece of onion. Cut each of the pastry-wrapped tenderloins into six 1-inch slices and arrange 3 on each plate. Sauce the lamb with the stock that remains in the pan. Garnish with chervil and serve immediately.

Lamb Stock

Bones from one 3 1/2-pound saddle
　　of lamb (the meat is used later in
　　the recipe), chopped into 2 pieces*
　　(approximately 2 1/2 pounds total)
2 quarts water
1 quart chicken stock
2 heads garlic, sliced in half horizontally
2 bunches thyme
2 bay leaves

Meat from saddle of lamb: 2 loins and
　　2 tenderloins
1 potato
5 Roma tomatoes
3 red onions, peeled
1/2 cup red wine vinegar
1 green zucchini
Salt and freshly ground black pepper
2 leaves brik pastry†
1 egg mixed with 2 tablespoons water,
　　for egg wash
3 to 4 tablespoons olive oil
Leaves from half a bunch of fresh oregano
2 cups Lamb Stock
12 fresh basil leaves
Chervil or parsley sprigs, for garnish

*Have your butcher bone the saddle of lamb and remove the fat and silverskin from the loin.

†Brik pastry is a Tunisian specialty, similar to phyllo dough, made of semolina flour, water and salt. A leaf is 12 inches in diameter and very thin; 2 leaves weigh approximately 10 grams. Phyllo dough may be substituted.

POACHED PEARS WITH CINNAMON AND VANILLA RISOTTO

Serves 4. Wine recommendation: a medium-sweet Muscat

Risottto

Risotto

3 cups milk

4 ounces (a heaping 1/2 cup) Arborio rice

1/4 cup sugar

2 vanilla beans, split

1/2 teaspoon ground cinnamon, plus
    extra for garnishing

4 pears, peeled but left whole

4 vanilla beans, split

2 cinnamon sticks

2 1/4 cups sugar

1 quart water

4 sprigs mint, for garnish

To make the risotto, place the milk, rice, sugar, vanilla beans and cinnamon in a saucepan over low heat. Cook, stirring frequently, for approximately 35 minutes, or until the rice is very tender. Remove the pan from the stove and let the risotto cool.

To poach the pears, place them in a deep saucepan with two of the vanilla beans, the cinnamon sticks and 1 1/4 cups of the sugar. Add water to cover, bring the liquid to a boil and cook the pears for approximately 30 minutes, or until they are tender. Set aside to cool. Then, with a melon baller, remove the core from the bottom of each pear. Slice the pears in half.

To make a syrup, combine the water with the remaining vanilla beans and sugar in a saucepan. Over medium heat, reduce the liquid by three-quarters, until you have 1 cup. Set the syrup aside to cool.

To serve, place a heaping 1/4 cup of risotto in the center of each plate. For each serving, slice up 2 pear halves lengthwise. Arrange the pears in a fan shape on top of the risotto, the slices curving outward like petals. Pour 1/4 cup of vanilla syrup on each pear and garnish with a sprig of mint; sprinkle ground cinnamon around the edge of the plate.

Tra Vigne Ristorante

Tra Vigne is one of the Napa Valley's most celebrated restaurants, but nothing you hear prepares you for the real thing. The entrance through a Mediterranean courtyard filled with olive trees, trellised vines, and crouching lions transports you at once to Italy. Within are high-ceilinged rooms worthy of a palazzo, with beaded lamps, wrought-iron railings, and a gleaming hand-carved bar. The effect is breathtaking, yet the food, for all its excellence, is surprisingly unpretentious.

"My family's roots are in Calabria, and I often find myself re-creating, in modern-day terms, the simple Calabrian food of my family," says Michael Chiarello, the chef and proprietor. The antipasti, for example, might include giant mushrooms sautéed simply in olive oil and garlic. The secret lies in the ingredients: mushrooms picked that day and olive oil pressed fresh to Chiarello's own specifications.

A surprising number of the restaurant's foodstuffs are made right on the premises, including prosciutto and pancetta, cheeses, breads, pastas, and cured olives. Many of these items are sold in the restaurant's cantinetta, which also has a full bar where you can get dark, flavorful espresso.

Chiarello merges the traditional cooking styles of Calabria and Tuscany with the ingredients available in California to create a cuisine that appeals to American palates. "Lifestyles in the valley are very casual," Chiarello explains, "and the local ingredients are full of flavor. Wine-country cooking is not about a way of cooking, but cooking amid a way of life."

GOAT CHEESE SALAD WITH OVEN-DRIED FIGS

Serves 4. Wine recommendation: a light, crisp Sauvignon Blanc or dry Riesling

Oven-Dried Figs

2 tablespoons unsalted butter

1 fresh bay leaf (dried is fine if fresh is not available)

1 tablespoon balsamic vinegar

1 teaspoon lemon juice

4 figs, halved

Salt and freshly ground pepper

2 ounces (1/4 cup) *pancetta*, diced

4 tablespoons extra virgin olive oil

6 cloves garlic, minced

2 teaspoons fresh thyme leaves

1/4 cup sherry vinegar

4 ounces goat cheese, cut into 4 pieces

4 cups *tatsoi* or baby spinach leaves

4 cups *frisée*

A Note on Procedure
Prepare the figs ahead of time; they will take up to 3 hours.

Oven-Dried Figs
Preheat the oven to 150 degrees F. Melt the butter in a saucepan over medium heat, and when it starts to turn brown, crumble in the bay leaf and add the balsamic vinegar and lemon juice. Arrange the fig halves in a shallow baking pan, spoon the browned butter over them and season with salt and pepper. Cook in the oven for 2 1/2 to 3 hours. The figs are done when the edges start to dehydrate and wrinkle, but the figs are still moist and not too chewy.

Render the *pancetta* in a small sauté pan over low heat until it releases half of its fat and has browned, approximately 5 minutes. Drain and reserve the fat.

Place the olive oil and 1 tablespoon plus 1 teaspoon of the reserved *pancetta* fat into a saucepan, over medium heat. If you do not have enough *pancetta* fat, add olive oil to make up the difference. When the oil is hot, but not smoking, add the rendered *pancetta*. When the *pancetta* starts to cook, add the garlic and brown it lightly; add the thyme and heat until you hear a popping or crackling sound. Deglaze the pan with the vinegar. With the pan still over the heat, add the goat cheese, and just when the cheese starts to melt, toss in the *tatsoi* and *frisée*, add the figs, season with salt and pepper to taste and serve warm.

Chicken Marinade
1/2 cup white wine
1 tablespoon thyme
1/2 teaspoon freshly ground black pepper
2 teaspoons garlic
1/2 cup extra virgin olive oil

6 half-breasts of chicken, skin still on

Chicken Spice Mix
1/2 teaspoon coriander seeds
1/4 teaspoon white peppercorns
1 tablespoon fennel seed
1 tablespoon kosher salt

1/2 cup butter

Potato and Pea Risotto
8 cloves garlic, minced
3 tablespoons olive oil
1 1/4 pounds baking potatoes, peeled and
    cut into 1/2-inch dice (approximately
    3 cups)
Salt and freshly ground black pepper,
    to taste
3/4 cup white wine
3 to 4 cups chicken stock
1 cup shelled and blanched English peas
    (approximately 1 1/2 pounds in
    the shell)
1 1/2 cups baby spinach leaves
1/2 cup freshly grated Parmesan cheese

CHICKEN BREAST WITH POTATO AND PEA RISOTTO*

Serves 6. Wine recommendation: a full-bodied Zinfandel, Merlot or Pinot Noir

Chicken Marinade
Combine the wine, thyme, pepper, garlic and olive oil in a small bowl.

Place the chicken breasts in a glass or ceramic dish, pour the marinade over the top and set the dish aside for 30 minutes at room temperature or 2 to 4 hours in the refrigerator. Turn the breasts occasionally.

Chicken Spice Mix
Grind the coriander seeds, peppercorns and fennel seeds finely and add the salt.

To cook the chicken, preheat the oven to 325 degrees F.
   Drain off the marinade and discard it. Melt the butter in an ovenproof dish. Sprinkle the chicken spice mix over the chicken breasts and place them in the dish, skin side down. Bake for 15 to 20 minutes until the chicken breasts are just cooked through.

Potato and Pea Risotto
While the chicken is cooking, prepare the risotto. In a heavy saucepan, cook the garlic over medium-low heat in the olive oil until it is soft and translucent. Add the diced potatoes, stir them to coat with oil, season with salt and pepper and pour in the wine. Reduce the wine to 1/4 cup and then add 3 cups of the chicken stock. Simmer the mixture for 10 to 15 minutes until the potatoes are cooked and the stock is reduced, but still slightly brothy, adding more stock if necessary. Add the peas and spinach and cook slowly for another minute, just to heat the peas through and wilt the spinach. Gently stir in the cheese.

To serve, remove the chicken from the ovenproof dish and pour off approximately two-thirds of the cooking liquid into the risotto, mixing it in gently. Place a portion of the risotto in the center of each plate, cut each half chicken breast into two and arrange the halves off center on top of the risotto.

*The name *risotto* refers here to the technique; potatoes, rather than rice, are used to create this risotto.

1 cup (2 sticks) unsalted butter

1 cup plus 2 tablespoons sugar

2 eggs, separated

8 ounces (1 1/3 cups) potato starch
(potato flour)

1/4 ounce *pane di angeli** (vanilla-flavored
Italian baking powder)

3 medium-sized pieces lemon zest, minced

1 teaspoon vanilla extract

1 1/2 teaspoons brandy

Fruit Topping

1 basket (1 pint) strawberries or
equivalent quantity of other fresh
fruit, hulled

1 tablespoon balsamic vinegar

2 tablespoons sugar

1 teaspoon lemon juice

Mascarpone or vanilla ice cream,
for garnish

*Pane di angeli is available in most Italian
grocery stores. Regular baking powder may
be substituted; use 1 1/2 teaspoons.

TORTA SABIOSA

One 10-inch cake; serves 8. Wine recommendation: a light, fruity, slightly sweet Muscat with low acidity and low alcohol

Preheat the oven to 350 degrees F. Butter a round 10-inch cake pan and line it with parchment paper.

Cream the butter and 1 cup plus 1 tablespoon of the sugar together in a mixer with a paddle for 5 minutes. Add the egg yolks, one at a time. Stir in the potato starch, *pane di angeli,* zest, vanilla and brandy. In a separate bowl, beat the egg whites with the remaining 1 tablespoon sugar until they form soft peaks. Fold the whites into the yolk mixture and pour the batter into the prepared pan. Bake for 45 minutes and do not open the oven! Remove the cake from the oven and let it cool in the pan for 30 minutes. Remove the cake from the pan before it cools completely.

Fruit Topping

Slice the fruit into bite-sized pieces and toss it in a bowl with the vinegar, sugar and lemon juice.

To serve, slice the cake and serve it with the fruit topping and garnish with a dollop of *mascarpone.*

Terra

If all you know of Terra is its name and its fieldstone Tuscan architecture, you might think that it's merely another Italian restaurant in a valley full of good ones. Terra does serve Mediterranean cuisine, but with two secret ingredients: Hiro Sone and Lissa Doumani.

"My family has grown sasanishiki *(premium rice) in Japan for eighteen generations," Sone says. "I still remember at the end of the day, when everyone had left the field, my grandmother picking up lost grains of rice from the ground. From her I learned my respect for food: Even a piece of rice should be treated with respect." Sone's first teacher was his mother; later instructors included the master chefs Roger Jaloux and Joël Robuchon.*

Sone met Doumani when they both worked at Spago in Los Angeles under Wolfgang Puck. Sone then returned to Japan to open a Spago in Tokyo, and Doumani followed. When they came back to California, the Napa Valley offered the ideal setting for the southern French/northern Italian/Asian restaurant they dreamed of. Although the building itself is listed in the National Register of Historical Places, today, its stone-and-timber interior, accented with soft lighting, modern art, and a copious wine rack, has the aura of a cozy neighborhood restaurant.

"An important part of our style is to make the connection between food and wine," explains Doumani, whose father owns Stags' Leap winery. "Situated in the middle of the wine country, we don't know if people come here first for the food or for the wine, but we know that the experience is linked. When a chef has a chance to make a special menu to go with specific wines, it is the pinnacle of dining."

20 ounces tuna loin, cut into a triangular
   wedge 2 inches wide on each side
1/3 cup dry *herbes de Provence*
1 tablespoon freshly ground black pepper
2 tablespoons olive oil

Sherry Balsamic Vinaigrette
2 teaspoons sherry vinegar
1 tablespoon balsamic vinegar
2 teaspoons Dijon mustard
2 teaspoons finely chopped shallots
2 tablespoons corn oil
1/4 cup extra virgin olive oil
Pinch of salt and freshly ground
   black pepper

Mustard Soy Vinaigrette
3 tablespoons whole-grain mustard
1 tablespoon soy sauce
1 tablespoon rice vinegar
2 tablespoons tomato *concassé* (peeled,
   seeded and finely diced fresh tomato)
1 tablespoon finely chopped chives
Pinch of freshly ground black pepper
2 tablespoons extra virgin olive oil

8 ounces (12 cups) baby greens
2 ounces (1 cup) *kiaware* (daikon sprouts)

TATAKI OF TUNA WITH FIELD GREENS AND MUSTARD-SOY VINAIGRETTE

Serves 6. Wine recommendation: a dry Sauvignon Blanc or sparkling wine

Dredge the tuna loin in the *herbes de Provence* and sprinkle with pepper. In a sauté pan, heat the olive oil over high heat, add the tuna and sear each side for approximately 10 seconds, just until the outer 1/4 inch of the fish turns white. Transfer the tuna loin to a baking pan and refrigerate.

Sherry Balsamic Vinaigrette
In a medium-sized mixing bowl, combine both vinegars, the mustard and shallots. Slowly add both oils to the vinegar mixture and whisk together. Season with salt and pepper.

Mustard-Soy Vinaigrette
In another medium-sized mixing bowl, combine the mustard, soy sauce, vinegar, tomato, chives and pepper and whisk in the oil.

To serve, toss the baby greens with the sherry balsamic vinaigrette. Place a portion of the tossed greens in the center of each plate. Slice the tuna 1/4 inch thick and arrange the slices around the greens. Drizzle the mustard-soy vinaigrette on the tuna and sprinkle *kiaware* on the greens.

GRILLED SALMON WITH CABBAGE, THAI RED CURRY SAUCE AND BASMATI RICE

Serves 6. Wine recommendation: a dry, full-bodied Gewürtztraminer, Riesling or young Pinot Noir

Preheat the oven to 350 degrees F.

Basmati Rice

In a small ovenproof saucepan, combine the *basmati* rice, water and butter. Bring the mixture to a boil and cover the pan with a lid. Put the rice in the oven and cook it for approximately 12 minutes. Keep warm.

Cabbage Salad

In a medium-sized mixing bowl, combine the cabbage, cucumber, cilantro and mint and set aside. The soy sauce and vinegar should be added just before serving.

Thai Red Curry Sauce

In a sauté pan over medium heat, heat the peanut oil and sauté the garlic and ginger until they are light brown. Add the coriander seeds, curry powder, Thai curry paste, paprika and cumin and sauté the mixture for approximately 2 minutes over low heat until the flavor gets stronger. Add the coconut milk, tomato purée, soy sauce and brown sugar. Bring the mixture almost, but not quite, to a boil, remove from the heat and keep warm.

Just before serving, preheat a grill to high or prepare a charcoal fire grill.

Brush the salmon with oil and season with salt and pepper. Grill the fillets for 1 1/2 to 2 minutes per side. Keep warm.

To serve, finish seasoning the cabbage by tossing it with the reserved soy sauce and vinegar. Spoon a portion of rice on the center of each plate and place a salmon fillet on the rice. Arrange the cabbage on the salmon and pour the sauce around it. Sprinkle with the peanuts and serve hot.

Basmati Rice

1 1/2 cups *basmati* rice
2 1/4 cups water
3 tablespoons unsalted butter

Cabbage Salad

4 cups very finely julienned cabbage, loosely packed
2/3 cup julienned, peeled and seeded cucumber, loosely packed
1/3 cup cilantro leaves, loosely packed
1/3 cup mint leaves, loosely packed
1 teaspoon soy sauce
1 tablespoon rice vinegar

Thai Red Curry Sauce

2 tablespoons peanut oil
1 tablespoon minced garlic
1 tablespoon minced ginger
2 teaspoons coriander seeds, cracked
1 tablespoon curry powder
2 teaspoons red Thai curry paste*
1 tablespoon paprika
2 teaspoons ground cumin
2 1/2 cups coconut milk*
5 1/3 tablespoons tomato purée
2 tablespoons soy sauce
1/4 cup brown sugar

Six 6-ounce salmon fillets, 3/4-inch thick
1 tablespoon olive oil
Salt and freshly ground black pepper
1/2 cup roasted peanuts, roughly chopped

*Available at any Thai market. The coconut milk may be fresh or canned—make sure that no sugar has been added.

SAUTÉED STRAWBERRIES IN CABERNET SAUVIGNON AND BLACK PEPPER SAUCE

6 tablespoons sugar

1 1/4 cups Cabernet Sauvignon

A quarter of a vanilla bean,
  split lengthwise

1 1/2 teaspoons cornstarch

4 cups strawberries

2 tablespoons unsalted butter

Pinch of freshly ground black pepper

Vanilla-bean ice cream, as an
  accompaniment

Serves 6. Wine recommendation: a Cabernet Sauvignon Port

In a medium-sized saucepan, bring the sugar, 1 cup of the wine and the vanilla bean to a boil. In a small mixing bowl, whisk the remaining 1/4 cup wine and the cornstarch together, then slowly whisk this mixture into the boiling sugar and wine mixture. Remove the mixture from the heat and set aside.

Hull the strawberries and quarter them lengthwise.

To serve, melt the butter over high heat in a medium-sized sauté pan and sauté the strawberries for 1 minute. Add the wine sauce and the pepper, bring the liquid to a boil and simmer for 10 seconds. Divide the strawberries and sauce among 6 serving bowls, garnish each bowl with a scoop of vanilla-bean ice cream and serve immediately.

The Model Bakery

Sometimes old ways are still the best. In the 1920s, Italian stonemasons built huge brick ovens for a bakery on Main Street in downtown St. Helena. The 14-by-18-foot ovens were made for hearthstone baking, in which breads are placed directly on the stone, and the temperature is controlled by the amount of air fed to the fire. Seventy-five years later, the Model Bakery is using these same ovens, in the same way, to produce award-winning breads and baked goods that are sold on the premises and also to Terra, Brava Terrace, Meadowood, and other leading restaurants and wineries in the valley.

"Baking directly on the hearth gives the bread a crust that is unique," says the owner, Karen Mitchell. The Model Bakery's signature sourdough breads include a pain du vin, *made from whole wheat and a wine-grape "mother" (starter). There are also sweet French loaves and breads of cracked wheat, rye, oatmeal, brown rice, and polenta. Desserts created by the pastry chef Marsha Huber range from fresh fruit tarts and cakes to the bakery's own Chocolate Rad ("as in radically chocolate") cookie. Everything, sweet or savory, is made with organic flour.*

The bakery's morning lineup includes a wide range of croissants, pastries, coffee cakes, and muffins. If one of these isn't enough to rev you up, ask for an espresso or caffè latte to go with it. A little later in the day, you can indulge in something stouter, such as a freshly made sandwich or an individual pizza.

Caramel Sauce

1 cup sugar

Approximately 1/8 cup water

1 cup heavy cream, slightly warmed

Ganache

16 ounces bittersweet chocolate

1 cup heavy cream, slightly warmed

3 tablespoons unsalted butter

2 1/4 cups cake flour

1/2 cup plus 2 tablespoons unsweetened
 cocoa

1/2 teaspoon baking powder

1 1/4 teaspoons baking soda

1 teaspoon salt

3/4 cup (1 1/2 sticks) unsalted butter

1 2/3 cups sugar

3 eggs

1 1/3 cups strong coffee, freshly brewed
 and cooled

1/2 cup toasted pecans, roughly chopped
 (save 10 good-looking halves for
 decoration)

TURTLE CAKE

Makes one 8-inch cake

A Note on Procedure

Make the caramel sauce and the *ganache* the day before.

Caramel Sauce

Put the sugar into a small, heavy saucepan and slowly add water until it resembles wet sand. Cook over medium heat, washing down any sugar crystals from the sides of the pan with a small brush dipped in cold water. Cook the sugar until it caramelizes to a golden brown. While the syrup is still on the heat, slowly add the slightly warmed cream. Continue to cook the mixture over low to medium heat until it thickens, approximately 20 to 25 minutes. Pour the sauce into a heatproof bowl and let it cool on the counter for approximately 1 hour before covering and refrigerating overnight. (The warm sauce is thin, but will thicken when refrigerated.)

Ganache

Chop the chocolate into small pieces. Scald the cream and butter by combining them in a small saucepan and heating the mixture over medium heat until it is just about to boil. Turn the heat to low and add the chopped chocolate, stirring to incorporate, until the mixture is smooth. Remove the pan from the heat, put the ganache into a heatproof bowl and let it cool. Then cover with plastic wrap and refrigerate it overnight.

To make the cake, preheat the oven to 350 degrees F and butter and line with parchment 3 round, 8-inch cake pans.

Sift together the flour, cocoa, baking powder, baking soda and salt. In a separate bowl, cream the butter and sugar until fluffy. Add the eggs one at a time. Scrape down the bowl to incorporate the ingredients. Alternately add the coffee and the flour mixture. Scrape down the bowl again and beat the mixture on medium speed for approximately 2 minutes.

Divide the batter evenly among the 3 pans and bake the cakes for 35 to 40 minutes or until a cake tester comes out clean. Let the cakes cool in the pans for 15 minutes, then turn them out onto racks to cool completely.

When you are ready to assemble the cake, remove the *ganache* from the refrigerator. It can be softened by putting it into a mixing bowl and beating it with a paddle. If it needs to be softened further, put it in a bowl of warm water for approximately a minute.

Using a serrated knife, trim all 3 cake layers so that they are flat. Put the bottom layer on an 8-inch circle of cake cardboard. Cover the cake with a thin, even layer of *ganache*. Put the second cake on top, and using a plain no. 3 tip, pipe a ring of *ganache* around the outer edge of the cake. This will act as a dam for the caramel center. Spoon a layer of caramel inside the *ganache* ring. Sprinkle a layer of chopped pecans over the caramel and place the third cake layer on top.

Cover the entire cake with a thin layer of softened *ganache*, smoothing the sides and top. With the no. 3 tip, make 10 "turtles"—oval rosettes—around the top of the cake. Place a toasted pecan half in each rosette at a jaunty angle.

Keep the cake refrigerated until 1 hour before serving.

WALNUT BREAD

Makes two 1/4-pound loaves

1 cake fresh yeast or 1/2 tablespoon active
    dry yeast (do not use fast-acting yeast)

1 1/4 cups water

1/4 cup honey

2 tablespoons canola or walnut oil

4 cups bread flour

1 1/2 teaspoons salt

1 1/2 cups toasted walnut pieces

In a small bowl, dissolve the yeast in the water. Whisk in the honey and oil. Place the flour and salt in a large bowl (if you are using a mixer, use a dough hook) and slowly add the liquid ingredients, mixing at low speed. Add the walnuts. At a higher speed, knead the dough until it is smooth. If you are mixing by hand, turn the dough onto a floured work surface, add the nuts gradually, and then knead the dough for 10 minutes by hand.

Put the dough into a clean, lightly oiled bowl and cover it with plastic wrap. Set the bowl aside in a warm place to rise. This may take up to 3 hours; the dough will double in size. Punch down the dough and divide it into 2 large pieces. Shape each into a round loaf. Put the loaves onto parchment-lined baking sheets and allow them to rise a second time, for approximately 30 minutes or until the dough springs back when pressed with a finger.

While the loaves are rising, preheat the oven to 350 degrees F. Slash the top of the loaves with a sharp knife, making 2 or 3 cuts, and, if you like, dust each loaf with extra flour. Bake the loaves for 40 to 45 minutes, until they are nicely brown and firm. This bread looks dark in color, although no whole wheat flour is used, since the walnuts release a dark oil when cooked.

Brava Terrace

One Thanksgiving day long ago, nine-year-old Fred Halpert was asked to mind the turkey. The next year, he cooked the turkey himself on the backyard barbecue. Three years later, he was cooking turkeys for the neighborhood. Today, Halpert is the chef and proprietor of Brava Terrace in St. Helena, and he's still barbecuing: Every Tuesday he hosts "Ribs and Zin Night," when he serves large platters of barbecue with a selection of local Zinfandels offered by the tumbler. He also makes his own barbecue sauce, using Scotch Bonnet chile peppers that he grows himself.

"The dream of every chef is to own his own restaurant, especially in the wine country," Halpert says. He found his dream in 1990, when he left the Portman Grill in San Francisco. "The wines, the fresh herbs and produce, and the terrain of Napa all reminded me of southern France."

Halpert's memories of France include his training with such immortals as Alain Chapel and Roger Vergé. "Provençal cooking doesn't mask flavors, it opens up possibilities," he says. "That's why my menus have lots of fresh herbs for their bright tastes." Many of those herbs, and a variety of organic vegetables, come from the restaurant garden.

Halpert's clientele often includes world-class wine makers. "Wine makers travel all over and see a lot of food," he observes. "They want food that goes well with their wines." To satisfy these demanding customers, Halpert himself designs the wine list at Brava Terrace.

Adjacent to the restaurant is the spacious terrace that gives Brava Terrace its name. On a sunny day, the sun-splashed terrace is thronged with diners, taking in the vineyard vistas and the hearty food Halpert calls "the cuisine of the sun."

PROVENÇAL SALAD WITH MARINATED GOAT CHEESE

Serves 8. Wine recommendation: a Chardonnay with a crisp, citrus finish

A Note on Procedure
The goat cheese requires 3 days of marinating before serving.

Marinated Goat Cheese
Combine the olive oil, rosemary, thyme, garlic, bay leaf and peppercorns in a medium-sized bowl and marinate the cheese for a minimum of 3 days in the refrigerator. Drain the cheese and reserve the marinade.

Tear the lettuces into bite-sized pieces and wash and dry them.

To prepare the dressing, mix the olive oil, lemon juice, vinegar, two-thirds of the shallot and two-thirds of the chives in a small bowl and season with salt and white pepper.

Preheat the oven to 400 degrees F.

Place half a slice of the marinated cheese on each piece of bread and top with the remaining shallots. Drizzle with some of the marinade and heat in the oven for 3 minutes.

To serve, toss the lettuces with the dressing and arrange on plates. Place 2 cheese croutons on each plate, garnish with the remaining chives and serve at once.

Marinated Goat Cheese
1 cup olive oil
1 sprig rosemary
1 sprig thyme
2 cloves garlic, peeled
1 bay leaf
20 black peppercorns
8 ounces goat cheese, sliced into 8 pieces

1 pound assorted lettuces, such as
    green-leaf, red-leaf or Boston lettuce
1/2 cup olive oil
1/2 tablespoon lemon juice
1 1/2 tablespoons balsamic vinegar
1 shallot, finely chopped
1 bunch chives, finely chopped
Salt and white pepper, to taste
16 slices bread, cut diagonally from
    a baguette

CASSOULET OF LENTILS
WITH CHICKEN, SAUSAGE AND PORK

Serves 8. Wine recommendation: a Merlot with cherry, spice and soft tannins

1 carrot

1 medium yellow onion

2 stalks celery

1/4 cup olive oil

2 cups (1/2 pound) green lentils,
    preferably the French *lentilles du Puy*

1 bay leaf

2 sprigs thyme

5 cups chicken stock

4 half-breasts of chicken, boned and
    skinned

1 pound pork loin

Salt and white pepper, to taste

1 pound specialty link sausage
    (such as duck, venison or other game)

1 pound mushrooms, quartered

2 tablespoons unsalted butter

1 bunch chives, chopped

Dice the carrot, onion and celery. In a large pot, heat the olive oil and sauté the vegetables over medium heat. Add the lentils, bay leaf and thyme and continue to sauté for approximately 1 minute.

Add the chicken stock, bring the mixture to a boil, then cover. Stirring occasionally, cook for 15 minutes on medium heat or until the lentils are cooked al dente. Remove the pan from the heat and set aside.

Cut the chicken breasts and pork loin in half. Season with salt and pepper. Heat a dry, nonstick 12-inch skillet and sear the pork, then the chicken and then the sausages. Wipe out the pan with a paper towel and sauté the mushrooms in the butter until soft.

Quarter the chicken and pork pieces. Cut the sausages in half.

Return the pan containing the lentils to the heat. Add the chicken, pork, sausages and mushrooms to the lentils and cook until the meats reach the desired degree of doneness (2 minutes for rare; 4 for medium; 6 for well-done). Remove the bay leaf and thyme stems and season with salt and pepper to taste.

Ladle into 8 bowls and garnish with the chives.

FRESH FRUIT WITH ENGLISH CREAM AND MINT

Serves 8. Wine recommendation: a light, flowery late-harvest Riesling or Muscat

English Cream

1 vanilla bean

2 cups milk

4 egg yolks

1/2 cup sugar

4 cups assorted fresh fruit (such as
    strawberries, oranges, grapefruit,
    melon or berries) peeled, cored
    and seeded, as appropriate

8 sprigs mint, julienned

English Cream

Split the vanilla bean in half, scrape out the seeds and add them, along with the milk, to a medium-sized pot. (Discard the pod.)

Over medium heat, bring the milk to a boil, then remove from heat and set it aside.

In a medium-sized bowl, whisk the egg yolks and sugar together until the mixture lightens in color. Add one-third of the boiled milk and whisk thoroughly. Pour this mixture back into the remaining two-thirds of the milk and return the pot to the heat. Heat the mixture until it thickens, approximately 1 minute. Do not allow it to boil. Immediately strain the mixture and set it aside to cool.

Mix the prepared fruit and place in a serving bowl. Pour the English cream over the top and garnish with the mint.

All Seasons Cafe and Wine Shop

History is all on the side of Mark Dierkhising, the chef and co-owner of the All Seasons Cafe in Calistoga, at the north end of the Napa Valley. He has been cooking in the valley, and tasting its wines, for nineteen years—a long time by local standards. The All Seasons Cafe is housed in a building that was a hotel at the turn of the century and retains its charm with checkerboard tiles on the floor and fans on the ceiling.

Dierkhising is a third-generation purveyor of food and drink, following in the footsteps of a restaurant-owning father and a saloon-keeping grandfather who imported California wines to Minnesota as early as 1890. Mark and his brothers own something of a monopoly in Calistoga. They also own the Silverado Restaurant and Tavern, which opened in 1976, across the street.

Dierkhising's cooking, though, is as fresh as the day's delivery from Forni, Brown and Welch, one of the valley's excellent providers of fresh produce. Blending food and wine into a perfect meal is Dierkhising's passion, and the All Seasons Cafe stocks an impressive collection of vintages in its own wine shop on the premises. Dierkhising serves an unusually large number of wines by the glass, and he creates new dishes with specific wines in mind.

A grilled rabbit served with a plum, apple, and juniper berry sauce, for example, might be inspired by a fruity red Cabernet; a fresh seafood pasta with capers and black olives might be designed to complement a crisp young Sauvignon Blanc. Even the breads and desserts are made with the meal in mind, since they are produced in the Cafe's own bakery and ice creamery.

FIELD GREENS WITH BRAZIL NUT OIL VINAIGRETTE

1/2 cup organic Brazil nut oil*
1/4 cup raspberry vinegar
2 tablespoons chopped shallots
2 tablespoons chopped parsley
Salt and freshly ground black pepper,
    to taste
4 ounces (10 cups) loosely packed field
    greens, such as arugula, oak leaf,
    watercress or *frisée*

*Brazil nut oil is available from health
food stores; olive oil may be substituted,
but the taste is entirely different.

Serves 4. Wine recommendation: a full-bodied Pinot Noir or premier cru white Burgundy

Whisk the oil, vinegar, shallots, parsley and salt and pepper together in a bowl. Dress the greens with the amount of dressing that you prefer. Divide the salad evenly among 4 plates and serve.

1/4 cup olive oil

1 sprig tarragon

2 sprigs thyme

1 teaspoon freshly ground black pepper

1 tablespoon balsamic vinegar

4 boneless duck breasts, weighing
   2 to 3 pounds total

Wild Rice Yam Cakes

1/2 cup peeled and grated yam

1/2 cup peeled and grated russet potato

1 cup cooked wild rice

3 tablespoons diced red onion

3 green onions, minced

1 teaspoon ground nutmeg

1/2 teaspoon salt

Freshly ground black pepper, to taste

2 eggs, slightly beaten

2 tablespoons buckwheat flour

3 tablespoons all-purpose flour

Olive oil, for frying

Huckleberry Sauce

1 tablespoon chopped shallots

1/2 cup duck or chicken stock

3 tablespoons wild huckleberries

1 tablespoon unsalted butter

Salt and freshly ground black pepper,
   to taste

BREAST OF DUCK WITH HUCKLEBERRY SAUCE AND WILD RICE YAM CAKES

Serves 4. Wine recommendation: a rich, buttery Zinfandel or full-bodied Merlot

A Note on Procedure

The duck requires a minimum of 2 hours to marinate before cooking.

In a large nonreactive bowl, combine the oil, tarragon, thyme, pepper and vinegar. Add the duck and marinate for 2 hours at room temperature or overnight in the refrigerator.

Wild Rice Yam Cakes

While the duck breasts are marinating, prepare the wild rice yam cakes. Rinse the grated yam well with water and squeeze it dry. Rinse and squeeze the grated russet potato. Mix the rice, yam, potato, red onion, green onion, nutmeg and salt and pepper together in a bowl. Fold in the eggs. Fold in the flours, using additional flour to bind, if necessary. Shape the mixture into eight 4-inch-round cakes and fry them in a nonstick pan in olive oil over medium-high heat until they are brown, approximately 2 minutes per side. Keep warm in a low oven. *Serves 4.*

Drain the breasts, discarding the marinade. In a large sauté pan over low heat, with no additional oil or butter, sauté the duck, skin side down, until the skin is crisp; this will take 10 to 15 minutes. Periodically discard the fat that accumulates in the pan. When the skin is crisp, turn the breasts and sauté the second side just to sear. Remove the duck from the pan and keep it warm. Discard all the fat from the pan.

Huckleberry Sauce

Add the shallots and sauté for 1 minute. Add the stock, huckleberries and butter. Reduce the mixture by half, to a light glaze, and season with salt and pepper.

To serve, place 1 duck breast on each of 4 plates. Ladle the sauce over the top and serve with the wild rice yam cakes.

FLOURLESS CHOCOLATE COCONUT CAKE

10 ounces bittersweet chocolate,
  chopped small

2 ounces unsweetened chocolate,
  chopped small

4 tablespoons unsalted butter

1 cup heavy cream

5 eggs

1/4 cup sugar

1 cup toasted coconut

2 tablespoons Grand Marnier liqueur

Makes one 9-inch cake. Wine recommendation: a tawny Port or late-harvest, fortified Australian Muscat

Preheat the oven to 425 degrees F. Butter and flour a round, 9-by-1 1/2-inch cake pan.

Combine the chocolates in a medium bowl and set aside. Combine the butter and cream in a heavy saucepan and bring the mixture to a boil. Remove the pan from the heat and add the mixture to the chocolate, whisking until the chocolate is completely smooth.

Place the eggs and sugar into a bowl set over simmering water (a bain-marie) and whip for a minute or two until the mixture is thick and frothy and you cannot feel the sugar granules. Remove the mixture from the heat and continue to whip until it is thick and cool, 3 to 4 minutes. Fold in the coconut and liqueur just until they are incorporated. Fold in the chocolate mixture.

Turn the batter into the prepared cake pan and set the pan in a larger ovenproof pan into which you have poured enough hot water to reach halfway up the cake pan. Place in the oven, then immediately turn the oven down to 225 degrees F and bake the cake for 1 1/4 to 1 1/2 hours or until slightly firm on top.

Remove the pan from the oven and cool the cake completely in the refrigerator. To remove the cake from the pan, slightly warm the bottom of the pan on a stove burner before turning the cake out. The cake is best served at room temperature.

Catahoula Restaurant and Saloon

The covered plank sidewalks and rough-hewn storefronts of Calistoga may remind you of the stage set for a Western movie. But once you step into the industrial-chic interior of Catahoula and catch a scent of its southern, bayou cooking, you'll forget all about the Old West. The enormous mural in the restaurant and steel sculptures in the saloon, all by local artists, quickly draw you into an atmosphere that is modern and original.

That feeling extends right down to the food. Jan Birnbaum, who was previously the executive chef at the five-star Campton Place in San Francisco and is an alumnus of Paul Prudhomme's legendary K-Paul's restaurant in New Orleans, has turned his creativity loose at Catahoula to invent dishes such as rooster gumbo, jalapeño-pecan catfish, and balsamic duck with chile potatoes. Homey desserts, such as mango and blackberry upside-down cake and apple butterscotch grunt, are created by the pastry chef Sherry Yard, who worked with Birnbaum at Campton Place.

Birnbaum calls his cuisine "southern-inspired American," and for good measure he named the restaurant after the state dog of his native Louisiana. "Food doesn't have to be hot, but it has to be exciting in your mouth," he says. "It has to make you want to take the next bite."

If the dining room is full or your appetite needs whetting, you might want to try the saloon menu, which includes pizzas and salads along with more adventurous offerings such as crawfish tamales, green chile and polenta pie, and homemade wild boar sausage. And if you've tasted enough wine for one day, just ask the bartender for a Catahoula Cooler, a house-made carbonated lemonade mixed with freshly picked mint and smooth Southern Comfort.

SOFT-SHELL CRABS WITH VEGETABLE SLAW AND RÉMOULADE

Serves 12. Wine recommendation: a crisp, fruity, well-balanced Sauvignon Blanc or moderately dry Gewürztraminer

Rémoulade

Place the egg yolks, mustard, vinegar, lemon juice, pepper, salt, capers, onions, celery, Tabasco and shellfish reduction in a food processor and process for 1 minute. Do not let the mixture sit for too long before processing, since the salt and acid will denature the proteins in the eggs. Add the oils, in a drizzle at first, and then faster. Add tablespoonfuls of warm water as necessary to thin the sauce if it becomes too thick before all the oil has been incorporated. With a rubber spatula, fold in the parsley and tarragon and the crawfish tails, if using. Store the rémoulade in a covered container in the refrigerator until ready to serve. *Makes 3 cups.*

To cook the crabs, mix the flour with the kosher salt, cayenne, black pepper and paprika in a large bowl and set aside. In a separate bowl, beat the eggs and the milk.

Pour the frying oil into a deep sauté pan and heat to between 350 and 375 degrees F. Dust the crabs in the seasoned flour, making sure to get the flour under the flaps of the shell, and shake off the excess. One at a time, dip the crabs into the egg mixture and then back into the seasoned flour.

Place each crab carefully into the pan of hot oil (the crabs should be put in one at a time and can be fried in batches). Over moderate heat, fry the crabs first for 2 to 3 minutes on one side and then for 2 to 3 more minutes on the other side until they are golden brown. Remove the crabs to paper towels to drain.

Vegetable Slaw

Heat the oil in a sauté pan. The slaw may need to be cooked in batches. Quickly, over high heat, sauté the zucchini, bell pepper, onions and fennel. Add the parsley, lemon juice and salt and pepper.

To serve, place the slaw on a large platter, cut the crabs in half and arrange over the slaw. Drizzle the crabs with some of the rémoulade. Serve the remaining rémoulade in a side dish for dipping.

Rémoulade

2 egg yolks
1 teaspoon Dijon mustard
1 teaspoon Champagne vinegar
2 teaspoons lemon juice
Pinch of ground white pepper
Pinch of kosher salt
1/4 cup capers, drained
1/4 cup chopped onion
1/4 cup chopped celery
5 dashes Tabasco sauce
1 cup shellfish stock that has been reduced to 1/2 cup, or 1/2 cup bottled Atlantic clam juice
1 cup peanut oil
1/2 cup olive oil
1/4 bunch parsley, chopped
1 teaspoon tarragon, chopped
1/2 cup cooked crawfish tails (optional)

3 cups flour
3 tablespoons kosher salt
1 1/2 tablespoons cayenne pepper
1 tablespoon ground black pepper
2 tablespoons Hungarian paprika
4 whole eggs
1 cup milk
1 quart peanut oil or other vegetable oil, for frying
6 extra-large jumbo soft-shell crabs, measuring between 5 to 6 inches from point to point of their shells

Vegetable Slaw

1/4 cup olive oil
2 yellow zucchini, cut into thin strips
2 green zucchini, cut into thin strips
1 red bell pepper, cut into thin strips
1 large red onion, thinly sliced
1 bunch green onions, thinly sliced
1 head fennel, thinly sliced
1 bunch flat-leaf Italian parsley, chopped
2 tablespoons lemon juice
Salt and freshly ground black pepper, to taste

WARM ROASTED RABBIT AND WHITE BEAN SALAD WITH TOMATO CONFIT

Serves 8. Wine recommendation: an intensely fruity Zinfandel or spicy Pinot Noir

A Note on Procedure
The rabbit must be started two days in advance, the white beans the night before.

Combine the olive oil, thyme, rosemary, garlic and pepper in a bowl. Place the rabbit in a nonreactive vessel into which it fits tightly, pour in the marinade and marinate the rabbit in the refrigerator for 48 hours, rotating the pieces every 6 to 8 hours to expose them evenly to the marinade.

White Beans
In a large pot over medium heat, render the bacon in the olive oil until it is almost crisp. Add the carrots and onion and sauté until they are soft. Add the drained beans, bay leaf, cumin seeds, garlic, vinegar, black and red pepper and stock. Cook, covered, until the beans begin to soften. This will vary according to the type of bean used, from 40 minutes to 2 hours. Add the salt and continue to simmer, uncovered, until the beans are soft. Remove the bacon and bay leaf and set the beans aside.

Tomato Confit
Preheat the oven to 250 degrees F. Remove the stem and flower tips from the tomatoes with a sharp paring knife. Cut the tomatoes horizontally into 1/2-inch-thick slices. Spread the oil, salt, thyme and pepper over a baking sheet. Arrange the tomato slices on the sheet and bake for 1 hour. Remove from the oven, allow the tomatoes to cool and set them aside.

To cook the rabbit, preheat the oven to 350 degrees F. Pat the rabbit pieces completely dry. In a large, heavy roasting pan, sear them in the olive oil over moderate to high heat until they are evenly golden brown. Add the wine, stock, bay leaf, peppercorns and salt. Bring the ingredients to a boil on top of the stove, cover the pan and place it in the oven. Cook covered for 10 minutes, then remove the lid. Continue cooking, basting with the liquid at first every 15 minutes, more frequently toward the end of the cooking process. When the rabbit is done after approximately 1 hour, remove it from the pan and set it aside. The cooking juices should have thickened considerably and should be sticking to the surface of the meat like a glaze. If they are too thin, reduce them over high heat until you have 1/4 cup. When the rabbit is cool enough to handle, pick the meat into small, bite-sized pieces and set aside. Reserve the remaining liquid.

In a sauté pan, reduce the 1 cup of balsamic vinegar to 1/4 cup of syrup. Set aside.

Balsamic Vinaigrette
Place all the vinaigrette ingredients in a blender and purée until smooth and thick enough to coat a spoon. Do not overmix or it will become too thick, more like a mayonnaise.

Assemble the salad on a serving platter. Place the slices of *confit* in the upper left corner near the top of the platter. Place the beans, the rabbit pieces, 1/2 cup of the rabbit cooking liquid and 1/2 cup of the vinaigrette in a pan and bring to a boil. Pour the bean mixture into a large mixing bowl with the greens, season with salt and pepper and toss. Arrange the greens on the platter below the tomatoes. Drizzle the balsamic reduction over the salad and serve immediately.

1/2 cup olive oil
10 sprigs fresh thyme
6 sprigs rosemary
1 head garlic (top and skin removed), cut horizontally into 1/4-inch slices
1 tablespoon freshly ground black pepper
1 fryer rabbit (3 pounds), cut into pieces

White Beans
3 slices smoked bacon
1 tablespoon olive oil
2 carrots, cut into large dice
1 large onion, cut into large dice
1/2 pound (1 1/2 cups) large cannellini beans, soaked overnight in water
1 bay leaf
1/2 teaspoon cumin seed, toasted
6 cloves garlic, peeled and smashed
2 tablespoons red wine vinegar
1 teaspoon freshly ground black pepper
1/2 teaspoon red-pepper flakes
4 cups chicken stock
1 tablespoon kosher salt

Tomato Confit
4 Roma tomatoes
2 tablespoons virgin olive oil
1 teaspoon kosher salt
2 teaspoons chopped fresh thyme
1/2 teaspoon freshly ground black pepper

2 tablespoons olive oil
3/4 cup white wine
2 to 3 cups chicken or rabbit stock
1 California bay leaf
5 black peppercorns, smashed
1 teaspoon kosher salt
1 cup balsamic vinegar

Balsamic Vinaigrette
2 teaspoons balsamic vinegar
1/2 tablespoon sherry vinegar
1/2 cup extra virgin olive oil
1 clove garlic, minced
1/2 tablespoon minced shallot
Pinch of sugar

2 bunches arugula, washed and dried
1 head *frisée*, washed and dried

MANGO AND BLACKBERRY UPSIDE-DOWN CAKE

Makes one 10-inch cake; serves 10. Wine recommendation: a late-harvest Riesling

2 tablespoons unsalted butter,
  cut into peanut-sized pieces
1/3 cup brown sugar
2 tablespoons Amaretto liqueur
2 mangoes, peeled and cut into
  1/4-inch slices
1 basket blackberries

Batter
1 cup all-purpose flour
1/2 cup cake flour
2 teaspoons baking powder
1/2 cup (1 stick) unsalted butter
2 eggs
1 cup sugar

Ice cream or whipped cream,
  for accompaniment

Distribute the butter and sugar evenly over the bottom of a 10-inch-by-1 1/2-inch straight-sided cake pan. Drizzle the Amaretto over the top. Place pan over moderate heat on the range and melt the sugar, butter and Amaretto together. Allow the pan to cool until you can handle it. Arrange the mango slices lengthwise in concentric circles around the center of the pan, leaving a round hole in the center approximately 1 inch in diameter. Mound the berries over the center and set the pan aside.

Batter

Sift the flours and the baking powder together in a bowl. Melt the butter over medium heat in a saucepan until it turns the color of amber caramel. It will smell nutty, like hazelnuts, and is referred to as a *noisette*. Quickly remove it from the heat and pour it into a cool container to stop it from burning. Set aside.

Preheat the oven to 375 degrees F.

Whisk together the eggs and sugar in a stainless steel bowl for 2 minutes or until fluffy. Use open, upward motions to add the maximum amount of air. Using a rubber spatula, alternately mix in the dry ingredients and *noisette* in 3 or 4 additions. Do not overmix. Pour the batter directly over the fruit in the cake pan and bake for 50 to 60 minutes or until a toothpick comes out clean. Allow the cake to cool slightly for 5 to 10 minutes. Turn the cake onto a serving plate while it is still hot.

Serve the cake with ice cream or whipped cream, flavored with a few tablespoons of late-harvest Riesling.

Sonoma County

Ristorante Piatti

It was not so long ago that a visit to the Napa Valley meant leaving fine dining behind in the city. Then San Francisco restaurateur Claude Rouas opened Ristorante Piatti in the mid-valley town of Yountville. Its big windows, tiled floor, and open kitchen serving up regional Italian food made with fresh California ingredients were a hit with locals and visitors alike. The floodgates opened.

Now there are dozens of fine restaurants throughout the wine country, including another Piatti in the historic El Dorado Hotel on the plaza in the town of Sonoma. Presiding over the kitchen there is Doug Lane, who cooked his way west from his native New York until he reached San Francisco and became sous chef at Kuleto's. He then jumped to La Varenne in Paris before coming to the wine country.

"One of the beautiful things about Italian cooking is that usually there aren't a lot of different ingredients in one dish," he points out. "This enables the cook not only to extract the maximum flavor from each item but also to present a product that is as pleasing to the eye as it is to the palate."

Lane's flavorful dishes often play with the Italian national colors of red, green, and white: A salad of escarole and radicchio, for example, contrasts deep red and glossy green; a spicy red sauce on spaghettini may be studded with green olives and white pine nuts.

"During the summer, I use lettuces, berries, corn, and grapes and in fall and winter, the heartier crops such as chard, leeks, and radicchio," Lane says. "The many organic farms in Sonoma produce a myriad of fresh produce, and the farmers help me immensely in planning menus."

INVOLTINI WITH GOAT CHEESE AND BASIL

Serves 6. Wine recommendation: a lively Barbera

Marinara Sauce

1/4 cup plus 2 tablespoons olive oil

1/4 cup garlic cloves, peeled and crushed

3 cans (28 ounces each) pear tomatoes,
  drained and crushed

1/4 cup plus 2 tablespoons fresh basil
  leaves

Salt and freshly ground black pepper,
  to taste

Sugar, to taste

1 teaspoon minced garlic

1 cup olive oil

1 large eggplant, cut lengthwise into
  six 1/2-inch-thick slices

12 basil leaves

1 cup goat cheese

1/2 cup basil, sliced thinly, for garnish

Marinara Sauce

Heat the olive oil in a large saucepan, add the garlic and cook it slowly over medium-low heat until it is a dark golden brown, approximately 5 to 8 minutes. Skim out and discard the garlic. Add the tomatoes and basil leaves, season with salt and pepper and simmer the mixture for 1 1/2 hours.

Purée the sauce in a blender and strain to remove the seeds, which are bitter. Season again with salt and pepper, and if the sauce is too acidic, add pinches of sugar until it tastes balanced. This sauce freezes well. *Makes 2 quarts.*

Prepare a grill and preheat the oven to 475 degrees F. Combine the garlic and oil in a small bowl and brush the mixture lightly on both sides of the eggplant slices. Cook the eggplant on a hot grill until it is soft. Let the slices cool, then line them up on a work surface. Place 2 basil leaves and 1 1/2 tablespoons of goat cheese on each slice. Roll the eggplant slices around the goat cheese. Fasten the roll with a toothpick and repeat the procedure until all the *involtini* are made. Arrange the rolls in an ovenproof pan large enough to hold them all in one layer, pour a little water (approximately 1/8 inch) in the bottom of the pan and cook uncovered until the goat cheese at both ends starts to get soft.

Remove the rolls from the oven and serve them over a thin layer of marinara sauce, garnished with the sliced basil.

PASTA SICILIANA

Serves 4 to 6. Wine recommendation: a deep, full-bodied Zinfandel

Siciliana Sauce

3/4 cup pitted green olives, coarsely
    chopped (stuffed green olives may
    be substituted)

3/4 cup kalamata olives, pitted and
    coarsely chopped

1/2 cup plus 2 tablespoons pecorino
    cheese, cut into small cubes

1/4 cup currants

1/2 cup pine nuts, toasted

1/4 cup chopped fresh herbs
    (parsley, mint, basil, oregano
    or any combination)

1 1/2 teaspoons minced garlic

1/2 teaspoon anchovy paste

1 medium shallot, chopped

1 tablespoon lemon juice

1 tablespoon balsamic vinegar

1 tablespoon rice vinegar

1/4 teaspoon cayenne pepper, or to taste

3/4 cup pure olive oil

3/4 cup extra virgin olive oil

1 pound spaghetti or linguine

Chopped parsley, for garnish

Siciliana Sauce

In a large bowl, combine the olives, cheese, currants, pine nuts and herbs and mix well. Add the garlic, anchovy paste, shallot, lemon juice, vinegars and cayenne and mix again. Stir in the oils.

Bring a large pot of salted water to the boil over medium-high heat and cook the spaghetti for 6 to 8 minutes while stirring with a fork to keep the pasta from sticking together.

While the pasta is cooking, heat the sauce in a sauté pan until it is just warm; do not melt the pecorino cheese. Drain the pasta and toss it with the sauce. Place in pasta bowls and garnish with the parsley.

POACHED PEARS WITH CARAMEL SAUCE, VANILLA GELATO AND ALMOND COOKIES

Serves 6. Wine recommendation: a vintage Port

Almond Cookies

Preheat the oven to 350 degrees F and line a baking sheet with parchment paper.

On a separate baking sheet, toast the almonds in the oven until they are golden brown and set them aside to cool. Leave the oven on.

With an electric mixer, cream the butter and sugar until light and fluffy. Beat in the egg and vanilla. Slowly add the flour and mix until the ingredients are combined.

With the back of a spoon, spread 2 tablespoons of the dough into a 4-inch circle on the parchment paper. Allow at least 6 inches for each cookie to spread. A baking sheet will accommodate 2 cookies at a time. Sprinkle the cookies with the toasted almonds. Bake the cookies for 10 to 15 minutes until they are golden brown.

While the first batch of cookies is in the oven, spread the batter out for the next batch on a sheet of parchment paper—the batter will not spread on a warm baking sheet. (You can use the parchment again when it has cooled.) Cool the cookies on a wire rack.

Poached Pears

Place the pears in a deep pot and cover with plenty of water. Add the sugar, cinnamon stick, cloves and lemon peel. Bring the liquid to a simmer. Poach the pears over low heat until they are tender, approximately 20 to 30 minutes.

Slice the pears in half and carefully remove the core. Slice the halves lengthwise, being careful to keep the tops connected so that the slices can be fanned out on the plate.

Caramel Sauce

In a heavy pot, combine the water and sugar. Cook over medium heat until the mixture turns a dark golden brown. Do not stir. Remove the pan from the heat and slowly whisk in the cream, gradually at first, until the mixture stops bubbling. Set aside and warm gently just before serving.

The sauce freezes well or will keep for 2 weeks, covered, at room temperature. *Makes 3 to 4 cups.*

To assemble the dessert, spread the warm caramel sauce onto individual plates, making sure that the sauce is spread out farther than the diameter of the cookie. Place a cookie on top of the sauce, fan out half a poached pear on top of the cookie, then place a dollop of vanilla gelato alongside the pear.

Almond Cookies

1 cup sliced almonds

3/4 cup (1 1/2 sticks) unsalted butter, softened

1/2 cup brown sugar

1/2 egg, beaten

1/4 teaspoon vanilla extract

1/2 cup plus 2 tablespoons flour

Poached Pears

3 small pears, peeled but left whole

1/2 cup sugar

1 cinnamon stick

3 whole cloves

Peel from 1 lemon

Caramel Sauce

1 cup water

3 cups sugar

2 cups heavy cream

Vanilla gelato, for topping

Eastside Oyster Bar and Grill

"Wine-country cooking exemplifies the relationship that chefs and farmers have built together," says Charles Saunders, the chef and proprietor of the Eastside Oyster Bar and Grill, located just off the central plaza in the town of Sonoma. Saunders learned to work with farmers and other food purveyors while cooking in Switzerland. "Shopping in the open market each day, I learned about meat from old Swiss-German butchers, about bread from the French baker, and about the essentials of produce from the Italian farmers."

Saunders blends these influences into his own version of California cuisine, which he created to please both "taste advocates who want food that gratifies the senses" and "health advocates who relate to food as fuel." The goal, he says, is to "provide both nourishment and excitement. It's a challenge I look forward to every day."

This varied background is on vibrant display in the chef's preparation of oysters: on the half shell with freshly grated horseradish, swimming in a creamy champagne chowder, pan-fried on a stacked vegetable salad, souffléd in their shells, or layered in a New Orleans–style po'boy. Other shellfish, seafood, poultry, game, and beef, together with fruits and vegetables from the restaurant's own garden, round out the fare.

The Eastside provides just the right ambiance for enjoying Saunders' cooking. Its tiled floors, bentwood chairs, and wainscoted walls echo earlier eras. In summer, the cobblestone courtyard in the back is one of the best places in Sonoma county to beat the heat. Afterwards, you can check out some music across the street at the Sunnyside Blues Bar and Coffee Club, also owned by Saunders.

EASTSIDE'S HANGTOWN FRY

Serves 6. Wine recommendation: a Viognier with peachy, floral characteristics

A Note on Procedure

The crêpes should be made up to a day ahead. The lemon vinaigrette and Sonoma mustard dressing should also be made several hours to a day ahead to allow time for the flavors to blend.

Corn Crêpes

In a medium-sized bowl, sift the flour, pepper and salt. Add the corn, eggs, cream, milk, butter and lemon zest and whisk until combined and smooth. Do not overbeat. Allow the batter to stand for 30 minutes.

Pour 1/4 cup of the batter into a small, 8-inch nonstick skillet, swirling it around to cover the bottom of the pan and pouring out any excess; this will ensure the thinnest of crêpes. (If you don't have a non-stick skillet, brush the bottom of saute pan with melted butter.) Cook over medium heat for 1 minute until light golden brown, then turn the crêpe over and cook the second side for 10 seconds. Transfer the crêpe to a plate and set aside. Extra crêpes may be stored in the refrigerator for up to 5 days.

Lemon Vinaigrette

In a small bowl, combine the lemon juice and vinegar and whisk in the oil. Season with salt and pepper. *Makes 2 1/3 cups.*

Sonoma Mustard Dressing

If desired, the flavor of this vinaigrette can be intensified by adding a mustard infused reduction of white wine. In a small heavy saucepan, combine the wine and the mustard seed and boil the mixture until the liquid is reduced by half, approximately 30 seconds. Strain through a fine sieve, discard the mustard seed and set the reduction aside.

In a mixing bowl, blend the mustards into the mayonnaise with a wire whisk. Add the vinegar, onion, yogurt and wine reduction, if using. Blend well and set aside. Extra dressing can be stored in the refrigerator for weeks. *Makes 3 1/2 cups.*

Salad

Lightly toss the carrots, beets and radish together in a mixing bowl. Set aside. In a small bowl, mix the bell peppers and set aside.

In a skillet over medium heat, cook the bacon until approximately half the fat has been rendered. Pour off the fat, raise the heat and continue cooking the bacon until it is crisp. Drain on paper towels, cut the slices into a medium dice and set aside.

Reheat the crêpes in a 350 degree F oven just before frying the oysters.

When you are ready to serve, heat the peanut oil over high heat in a skillet. Place the flour, buttermilk and semolina mixture in 3 separate bowls. Dredge the oysters in flour, dip them in the buttermilk, coat them in the semolina and flour mixture and fry them for 1 minute, turn, and fry on other side for 30 seconds, or until they are golden.

To serve, place a warm crêpe on each plate and stack 1/2 cup of the spaghetti-cut vegetables on the crêpe. Toss the mixed greens with 3/4 to 1 cup of lemon vinaigrette and place 1 cup of greens on top of the vegetables. Garnish with 2 tablespoons of the peppers and a sprinkle of bacon and mound 4 oysters on top. Drizzle 2 tablespoons of the Sonoma mustard dressing over the top of the oysters and around the sides of each plate.

Corn Crêpes

1 cup flour

2 teaspoons freshly ground black pepper

1 teaspoon salt

1/3 cup corn kernels (1 ear)

3 eggs

2/3 cup cream

1 3/4 cups milk

4 tablespoons unsalted butter, melted until brown

Zest of 1 lemon, coarsely chopped

Lemon Vinaigrette

3/4 cup lemon juice

1/4 cup Champagne vinegar

1 1/3 cups peanut oil

1/4 teaspoon salt and a pinch of freshly ground white pepper

Sonoma Mustard Dressing

1/8 cup white wine (optional)

1 tablespoon mustard seed (optional)

1/2 tablespoon whole-grain mustard

1/2 teaspoon dry mustard

1/4 teaspoon Dijon mustard

1 cup mayonnaise

1/8 cup Champagne vinegar

1 tablespoon finely diced red onion

1/2 cup plain, low-fat yogurt

Salad

1 large carrot, finely julienned

2 large beets, finely julienned

1 small Japanese radish (*daikon*), finely julienned

1/4 large red bell pepper, diced

1/4 large yellow bell pepper, diced

3 slices applewood-smoked bacon

2 cups peanut oil, for frying

4 cups flour

2 cups buttermilk

2 cups semolina mixed with 1 cup flour

6 cups mixed baby greens, washed and dried

24 oysters, shucked

Spiced, Smoked and Grilled Pork Loin with Tomatillo and Chayote Salsa and Soft Polenta

Serves 6. Wine recommendation: a spicy, dark-berry Zinfandel

A Note on Procedure
The salsa and the Navajo spices can be made a day ahead.

Tomatillo and Chayote Salsa

1 pound tomatillos
2 *chayotes*
1 jalapeño pepper, seeded and finely diced
1 red bell pepper, roasted, peeled and diced
1/4 cup coarsely chopped cilantro leaves
1 teaspoon toasted ground coriander seed
1/4 cup fresh lime juice
2 tablespoons dark rum
2 tablespoons chile oil

Tomatillo and Chayote Salsa
Preheat the oven to 350 degrees F. Toss the tomatillos with a little olive oil, salt and pepper and roast in the oven for 30 minutes or until softened, being careful not to char them. At the same time, toss the chayote in a little oil, and bake for 45 minutes or until tender. Roughly chop the roasted tomatillos and *chayote*. Combine them with the jalapeño, bell pepper, cilantro, coriander seeds, lime juice, rum and chile oil in a large ceramic bowl and allow to stand at room temperature for several hours. Warm the salsa slightly in a saucepan just before serving.

Navajo Spices

2 tablespoons cumin seed
1 tablespoon coriander seed
1 tablespoon red-pepper flakes
1 tablespoon fennel seed
1 tablespoon whole cloves
1 cinnamon stick
2 tablespoons dried juniper berries
1/3 cup pure *ancho* or ground chile powder
2 tablespoons Hungarian paprika
1/4 cup kosher salt

Navajo Spices
Heat the cumin seeds, coriander seeds, red-pepper flakes, fennel seeds, whole cloves and cinnamon stick in a pan over low to moderate heat until the aromas of the spices are perceptible (just a few minutes). Remove the spices from the heat, place in a spice grinder and grind to a medium to fine powder. Crush the juniper berries slightly with the flat side of a knife, then chop them finely. Place the ground spices, juniper berries, chile powder, paprika and salt into a medium-sized nonreactive bowl and mix.

The spice mix may be used for fish, poultry or vegetables. Stored in glass jar with a tight-fitting lid, it will keep for up to 2 months. *Makes 1 1/4 cups.*

4 pounds boneless center-cut pork loin
1 tablespoon salt
1 tablespoon freshly ground black pepper
1 tablespoon sugar
1/2 fresh pineapple, peeled and cut into
   6 slices, each 3/8 inch thick
1 tablespoon light brown sugar
1 teaspoon finely diced jalapeño pepper
1/4 cup fresh lime juice
2 tablespoons tequila
2 1/2 cups veal stock

Sprinkle the pork loin with the salt, pepper, sugar and Navajo spices. Set aside.

Meanwhile, marinate the pineapple. In a mixing bowl, combine the brown sugar, jalapeño, lime juice and tequila and add the pineapple slices; marinate for 30 minutes.

While the pineapple is marinating, heat the veal stock in a small, heavy pan over a medium heat and simmer until it is reduced to 1/2 cup; then set it aside, keeping it warm.

Soft Polenta

1/2 cup semolina flour
1/2 cup fine-ground polenta
1 cup heavy cream
1 1/4 cups chicken stock
Salt and freshly ground black pepper
2/3 cup coarsely grated dry aged
   Monterey Jack cheese

3 ears sweet white or yellow corn,
   not shucked

Soft Polenta
Whisk the flour and polenta together with the cream and chicken stock in a heavy-bottomed, medium-sized pot over moderate heat. Bring the mixture to a simmer and lower the heat. Stirring it occasionally, allow the polenta to cook for 20 to 30 minutes, adding water if the mixture becomes too dry. Season with salt and pepper, remove from the heat, add the cheese and stir well.

Prepare a wood-fired grill, and when it is ready, grill the pork for 12 to 15 minutes for medium rare, 16 and 18 minutes for well-done. When there is space on the grill, add the corn and grill for 6 to 8 minutes, rotating the cobs while they are cooking; also grill the marinated pineapple for 1 minute on each side. When the corn is cooked, shuck it and quarter the cobs. Set aside, keeping them warm. Also remove the pineapple and set aside.

To serve, place the polenta in a pastry bag without a tip. Pipe a circle of hot polenta onto the center of each plate. Fill the circle with the warm tomatillo and *chayote* salsa. Place pieces of the corn at the top of each plate so that it is partially touching the polenta. Place a slice of grilled pineapple next to the polenta and then a slice of pork loin over the polenta so that it is raised by the corn. Ladle 1 1/2 tablespoons of veal stock over the top of the meat and serve immediately.

Tart Shell
1/4 teaspoon salt
1/8 teaspoon baking powder
1 tablespoon sugar
1 1/2 cups flour
1/2 cup (1 stick) cold, unsalted butter,
    cut into chunks
6 to 8 tablespoons very cold water
1/2 teaspoon finely chopped lemon zest

1/4 cup seedless raspberry jam,
    at room temperature
1 tablespoon confectioners' sugar
1/3 cup marzipan
1 pound ripe Santa Rosa plums, pitted
    but not peeled and cut into 1/2-inch
    wedges
2 large eggs
2 tablespoons granulated sugar
1 tablespoon brandy
2/3 cup flour, sifted twice
2 tablespoons unsalted butter, melted

Brandy 'n' Spice Ice Cream
1 quart vanilla ice cream, softened
1/4 cup brandy
1/4 teaspoon ground nutmeg
Pinch of allspice
1/4 teaspoon freshly ground black pepper
1/2 teaspoon ground cinnamon

SANTA ROSA PLUM TART WITH BRANDY 'N' SPICE ICE CREAM

Serves 8. Wine recommendation: an orange Muscat

Tart Shell

In a large, stainless steel bowl, sift the salt, baking powder, sugar and flour together. Chop the cold butter into pea-sized pieces and incorporate them into the flour. Add the water, 1 tablespoon at a time, and add the zest. To form a dough, work the mixture with a minimum number of strokes, adding more water as necessary. Remove the dough from the bowl and press it into a flat disk. Wrap it in plastic wrap and refrigerate until the dough is firm, approximately 30 minutes.

Preheat the oven to 350 degrees F. Roll out the dough to approximately 1/8 inch thick and place in a tart pan that is 12 inches in diameter and approximately 2 inches deep. Line the shell with parchment paper and weight it down with beans or pastry weights. Partially bake the shell for 12 to 16 minutes. Remove the paper and weights and allow the shell to cool for approximately 15 minutes before filling it. Leave the oven on.

Spread the raspberry jam on the bottom of the tart crust. Sprinkle the confectioners' sugar onto a cool, dry surface and roll out the marzipan to a thickness of 1/8 inch. Place the rolled marzipan onto the bottom of the tart and trim it to fit the bottom of the shell. Arrange the plum wedges on top of the marzipan.

Place the eggs, sugar and brandy in a large bowl over a pot of boiling water, and using an electric mixer, beat the mixture for 2 minutes until it is warm to the touch. Remove the bowl from the heat and continue beating for another 4 minutes; the volume of the eggs should quadruple.

Using a rubber spatula and making big, wide strokes, alternately fold in the flour and melted butter. Ladle the mixture over the plums, allowing some of the fruit to remain exposed. Bake the tart in the oven for 20 to 25 minutes until it is a light golden brown. Allow the tart to stand for 10 to 15 minutes before serving it warm, accompanied by brandy 'n' spice ice cream.

Brandy 'n' Spice Ice Cream

In a nonreactive bowl, combine the ice cream with the brandy, nutmeg, allspice, pepper and cinnamon. Return the mixture to the freezer to become firm. *Makes 1 quart.*

The Grille at the Sonoma Mission Inn and Spa

The manicured grounds, curving drive, and ochre walls of Sonoma Mission Inn provide a preview of the restful, relaxing atmosphere of this world-class spa, a place where time seems to hover in a more elegant past. The spa's emphasis on health has been graciously integrated with a sensualist spirit—a combination exemplified by the cuisine of executive chef Mark Vann, who has united robust wine-country flavors with healthy low-calorie nutrition.

Vann's background ranges from a catering business in his native Texas to three years at The Pierre in New York City. When he came to the Sonoma Mission Inn in 1991, he saw an opportunity to balance the quality of local food-stuffs with the demands of his spa clientele.

"The first myth I like to shatter is that I'm the only one in the kitchen," he says. "It's not unusual for one of my sous chefs to come in with an armful of fresh beets from his garden, wanting to incorporate them into that night's menu." Vann himself is inclined to the same spontaneity, since he has an herb and vegetable garden at the Inn and a mushroom garden at home.

The Grille currently offers a spa menu and a regular menu at lunch and dinner, but Vann is looking ahead. "As time goes on," he says, "the two menus are getting closer to each other." Vann's basil-roasted chicken with artichokes and sun-dried tomatoes, for example, has lots of flavor but very little cholesterol. "People used to want spa cuisine to lose weight," Vann acknowledges. "Now they want it because it's good, healthy food."

WILD MUSHROOM BRUSCHETTA

Serves 4. Wine recommendation: a light-to-medium young Pinot Noir

Croutons

1 baguette French bread, sliced
    diagonally into 8 thin ovals, each
    approximately 6 to 8 inches long

4 tablespoons butter, melted

1/2 cup grated Parmesan cheese

2 tablespoons chopped fresh herbs,
    such as thyme or rosemary

Mushrooms

2 teaspoons olive oil

8 ounces wild mushrooms (such as a
    mixture of *shiitake,* oyster mushrooms
    and *chanterelles*)

2 cloves garlic, minced

1 sprig fresh sage, chopped

1 tablespoon Madeira

Salt and freshly ground black pepper,
    to taste

4 ounces fontina cheese, diced into
    1/2-inch cubes

1/2 cup peeled, seeded and diced tomato

1 teaspoon minced shallot

Croutons

Preheat the broiler. Place the slices of bread on a baking sheet. Brush one side with the butter. Top with the cheese and dust with herbs. Place the croutons under the broiler until the cheese melts, approximately 2 to 3 minutes. Leave the croutons on the baking sheet.

Mushrooms

Heat the oil in a pan over high heat. Add the mushrooms, garlic and sage. Sauté the ingredients until they are hot, add the Madeira and reduce the liquid by simmering for 5 to 7 minutes until it thickens. Season with salt and pepper.

To serve, arrange 2 croutons on a plate and distribute the mushrooms over the top of each crouton. Top with the fontina and place the croutons under the broiler to melt the cheese. Combine the diced tomato and shallot in a small bowl and garnish each crouton with some of the mixture.

SEARED NEW YORK STRIP WITH FOIE GRAS AND GARLIC MASHED POTATOES

Serves 4. Wine recommendation: a hearty Cabernet Sauvignon

Roasted Garlic
At least 1 head of garlic

Garlic Mashed Potatoes
5 potatoes (2 1/2 to 3 pounds), peeled
3/4 cup heavy cream
8 tablespoons unsalted butter
Salt and pepper, to taste

Horseradish Sauce
1 tablespoon minced shallots
1 tablespoon minced garlic
1 tablespoon minced thyme
1/2 cup brandy
2 cups veal or beef stock
1/2 cup cream
2 tablespoons prepared horseradish
   or 3 tablespoons peeled and grated
   fresh horseradish
Salt and pepper, to taste

1 cup thinly sliced carrots
2 tablespoons unsalted butter
2 tablespoons honey
4 New York strip steaks (each weighing
   10 ounces)
Salt and freshly ground black pepper
4 ounces Sonoma *foie gras,* cut into 4 slices
1/4 cup peeled, seeded and diced tomato,
   for garnish

Roasted Garlic

Because of its many uses and relatively long cooking time, we suggest that you prepare more than is needed for this recipe. Garlic may be roasted whole or in cloves. Roast whole garlic dry in a small, shallow pan in a 350-degree-F oven for 45 minutes to an hour. Some caramelized liquid may bubble out the top. To use, cut the heads in half horizontally and squeeze out the garlic pulp. Each head will yield between 2 and 3 tablespoons of pulp. Wrap well and store in the refrigerator.

An easier approach is to purchase already-peeled garlic cloves. Trim off the stem ends and toss the cloves in olive oil to coat. Place the garlic in a small baking dish, cover with foil and bake at 350 degrees F for 45 minutes to an hour. Each cup of raw garlic will yield approximately 1/2 cup of roasted pulp.

Garlic Mashed Potatoes

Cut the potatoes into chunks, boil them until they are soft and drain then thoroughly. While the potatoes are cooking, combine the cream, butter and 2 teaspoons of roasted garlic and heat the mixture over medium heat. Purée the potatoes using a ricer and place in a bowl. Add the warmed cream mixture and season with salt and pepper. Keep the potatoes warm.

Horseradish Sauce

Combine the shallots, garlic, thyme and brandy in a saucepan and simmer the mixture over low heat until it is reduced by half. (Caution: The reduction may flame.) Add the stock and cream and again reduce the mixture by half. Add the horseradish and season with salt and pepper. Keep the sauce warm.

In a small saucepan over medium heat, sauté the carrots for 5 minutes in the butter and honey and keep warm.

Prepare a hot grill. Season the steaks with salt and pepper and grill them for 4 minutes on each side for medium rare, 9 minutes for well-done.

To serve, spoon a portion of mashed potatoes onto the plate and place some carrots next to the potatoes. Lay the steak on top of the potatoes. Season the *foie gras* with salt and pepper and sauté in a dry pan over high heat for 30 seconds on each side; place a slice on top of each steak. Pour some of the horseradish sauce over the steak, top with diced tomato and serve.

WARM CHOCOLATE WAFFLES WITH ICE CREAM AND RASPBERRY SAUCE

1 1/4 cups (2 1/2 sticks) unsalted butter
3/4 pound bittersweet chocolate
6 eggs, separated
1/2 cup brown sugar
1/4 cup cognac
1 cup cake flour, sifted
1/2 cup granulated sugar

Raspberry Sauce
1 cup raspberries
2 tablespoons sugar
Juice of half a lemon (optional)

Vanilla ice cream, for accompaniment
Raspberries, for garnish

Serves 4. Wine recommendation: an orange Muscat

In a heavy pot or in the top of a double boiler, melt the butter and chocolate. In a separate bowl, whip the egg yolks and the brown sugar together. Cool the chocolate mixture slightly, for approximately 5 to 10 minutes, add it to the egg yolk mixture and combine. Add the cognac and flour, mixing with a wire whisk. Refrigerate the batter until it has thickened, approximately 2 hours.

Raspberry Sauce
Place the raspberries and sugar in the bowl of a food processor and purée. Taste and add lemon juice if necessary. Pass the mixture through a fine sieve to remove the seeds and set the sauce aside.

Preheat a well-greased waffle iron. In a bowl of an electric mixer, whip the egg whites until soft peaks form. Add the granulated sugar and whip slowly until the whites are firm but still moist. Whip the chocolate mixture until it is somewhat liquefied and stir in half of the egg whites. Fold in the remaining egg whites.

Cook the mixture in the waffle iron and serve the waffles immediately. Place a waffle on a plate, top with a spoonful of raspberry sauce and a dollop of ice cream and garnish with raspberries.

Kenwood Restaurant and Bar

A visit to the Kenwood Restaurant begins with a drive along the Sonoma Highway (Highway 12), through the north end of the Valley of the Moon. On a typical cool summer evening, you're likely to hear the sound of laughter and the clink of glasses as you pull into the parking lot. The two dining rooms often spill out onto the patio, and there is a constant parade of waiters carrying trays of food and pouring locally vinted wine.

The French-born owner, Maxime Schacher, and his American wife, Susan, opened Kenwood in 1987 and quickly found a following for Schacher's thoroughly modern cooking. Schacher honed his skills in the capitals of Europe and picked up his American inflections cooking at La Mirabelle and Chez Michel in San Francisco.

The combination of the full-flavored food and the romantic atmosphere the Schachers have created makes a dinner at Kenwood memorable. The decor is like Schacher's food: both comfortable and elegant. His background is in classical French cooking, but he has adapted the food for the wine-country palate and a more casual atmosphere. All his entrées, for example, include a sauce of some kind, but they are usually made with a reduction of the main ingredient rather than in the traditional French style.

Customers praise the gazpacho, the crab cakes, the authentic pommes frites *that accompany a juicy Sonoma beef burger, and any preparation of salmon. The wine list emphasizes Sonoma wineries, quite possibly owned or operated by someone seated at a nearby table.*

GAZPACHO

3 pounds ripe tomatoes, diced
1/2 cup peeled, seeded and diced cucumber
1/2 cup peeled and diced celery
1/2 cup peeled and diced onion
1/2 cup diced red bell pepper
8 sprigs fresh cilantro
1 small jalapeño pepper, seeded
1 clove garlic, peeled
2 leaves fresh basil
1 cup water
1 tablespoon olive oil
1 tablespoon vinegar
10 cumin seeds
1 teaspoon salt
Freshly ground black pepper, to taste

Serves 6. Wine recommendation: a rich, buttery Chardonnay or a shot of tequila

In a large bowl, mix together the tomatoes, cucumbers, celery, onion and bell pepper. Measure out 1 cup of the diced vegetables and set it aside along with 6 sprigs of cilantro for garnish.

Add the jalapeño, garlic, basil, the remaining cilantro, water, oil, vinegar, cumin seeds, salt and pepper to the remaining diced vegetables. In batches, purée the mixture in a food processor for 2 minutes and strain it through a medium sieve, reserving the liquid and discarding the solids. Chill for 30 minutes.

To serve the soup, ladle into six chilled bowls and garnish with the reserved diced vegetables and a sprig of cilantro.

Peppered Tuna with Papaya

4 ahi tuna steaks, each 1 to 1 1/2 inches
    thick and weighing 6 ounces
1 tablespoon coarse black pepper
1 tablespoon sesame seed oil
1 cup low-sodium soy sauce
1 tablespoon peeled and chopped ginger
1 papaya, peeled, seeded and diced
16 chives, for garnish
2 limes, cut in half, for garnish

Serves 4. Wine recommendation: a light, fruity Pinot Noir

Season the tuna with pepper. Heat the sesame seed oil in a sauté pan and over high heat sear the steaks, cooking for 20 seconds on each side; the tuna will be rare in the middle. Place each steak on a hot plate.

    In a separate pan over medium-low heat, warm the soy sauce, ginger and papaya. Pour the mixture over the tuna and garnish with the chives and lime halves.

Figs with Raspberry Coulis and Mint

2 cups raspberries
1/2 cup sugar
1 tablespoon lemon juice
8 black figs, halved
8 green figs, halved
4 sprigs mint, for garnish

Serves 4. Wine recommendation: a full-bodied Zinfandel

To make the *coulis*, purée 1 cup of the raspberries, the sugar and the lemon juice in a food processor for 2 minutes, then strain the mixture through a fine-meshed sieve.

    To serve, pour the *coulis* onto 4 chilled plates, arrange 4 fig halves of each color around the perimeter of the plate, pile 1/4 cup of the whole raspberries in the middle of each plate and garnish with a sprig of mint.

Willowside Cafe

A relative newcomer to the wine-country restaurant scene, the Willowside Cafe is easy to miss as you drive west from the highway north of Santa Rosa: It looks like a roadhouse dive, a pizza parlor, or a biker bar. In fact, it has been all three in its half-century of history. Today it's home to the friendly, full-flavored cooking of Richard Allen.

Allen, who has worked at Chez Panisse in Berkeley and at Domaine Chandon, starts his menu planning in the garden and then branches out across Sonoma Valley for the best the season has to offer. At Willowside, diners feast on local poultry and game, seasonal fruits and vegetables. "Wine-country cooking should showcase local farmers and ranchers and should also have a sense of place, like the wine," says the co-owner Michael Hale.

In fact, one of the best gardens in the area is Willowside's own, supervised by the co-owner and pastry chef Carole Hale. Carole was in charge of desserts and baking at Greens in San Francisco before the Hales launched Willowside in October 1993.

"Living in the country enhances your awareness of the seasons," Allen says. "It reminds you that time is passing." The cafe's low ceilings and hardwood floors keep it cozy in the winter, and overhead fans keep it cool in the summer. Copper-topped tables, bouquets of fresh flowers, and funky Americana from the nearby Jimtown store, provide cheerful accents year-round. The wine list includes selections from around the world, but emphasizes Sonoma wines which Allen and the Hales consider among the finest in the world.

HALIBUT IN CORN CRÊPES WITH TOMATO COULIS

Serve 4. Wine recommendation: a crisp, fruity Sauvignon Blanc

Crêpes

2 ears corn, husked (preferably Silver
    Queen or Platinum Lady)
1 cup less 2 tablespoons flour
1/2 teaspoon salt
1/2 teaspoon freshly ground white pepper
5 eggs, beaten
2/3 cup cream
1/3 cup unsalted butter, melted

Halibut

3 cups water
1 cup white wine or dry vermouth
2 bay leaves
1/2 pound halibut fillet
2 radishes, diced
1 lemon cucumber, diced (one-quarter of
    a peeled, diced cucumber plus 1 tea-
    spoon lemon zest may be substituted)
1 shallot, diced
2 sprigs thyme, chopped
3 tablespoons mayonnaise, preferably
    homemade
Salt and pepper, to taste

Tomato Coulis

1 tablespoon unsalted butter
Half a small yellow onion, cut into
    narrow strips
1 *serrano* chile, diced
2 vine-ripened tomatoes (we use Persimmon
    or Mandarin Gold), quartered
Salt and freshly ground white pepper,
    to taste
Pinch of sugar

Crêpes

Grill the corn over hot coals, giving the cobs a quarter turn, until the kernels are golden brown on all sides. (Watch the corn, not the clock.) Cut the kernels off the cob and set aside.

In a mixing bowl, combine the flour, salt and pepper. Make a well in the flour, add the eggs, whisk in the cream and then the butter. Add 1 cup of the corn, reserving the rest for garnish. Set the batter aside for 30 minutes.

Halibut

In a 12-inch skillet over medium-high heat, bring the water, wine and bay leaves to a near boil and poach the halibut fillet until the fish is opaque, approximately 7 minutes. Remove the halibut from the pan and set it aside to cool. When it is cool, flake the halibut into a bowl and toss with the radishes, cucumber, shallot, thyme and mayonnaise; season with salt and pepper to taste.

To cook the crêpes, pour 1/4 cup batter into a lightly buttered crêpe pan or an 8-inch nonstick skillet. Cook only one side and then stack the crêpes on a plate, separated by sheets of wax paper.

Tomato Coulis

Melt the butter in a nonreactive pan over low heat and add the onion. When the onion is soft, not browned, add the chile. Add the tomatoes, and when they release their juices turn heat to high and stir constantly. When the tomatoes have collapsed, remove from the heat and press the mixture through a food mill. If you don't have a food mill, pulse the mixture in a food processor and then push through a sieve. Season with salt and pepper. If too acidic, add a pinch of sugar. Set the *coulis* aside, keeping it warm.

To assemble the dish, preheat the oven to 400 degrees F. Place each crêpe, cooked side down, on a work surface and top with some of the halibut mixture. Roll the crêpes up, place on a baking sheet and bake in the oven for 5 minutes, removing the crêpes when the edges are crisp.

To serve, put the tomato *coulis* on a plate, place a crêpe in the center and garnish with the remaining corn.

Duck Stock

1 duck weighing approximately
    5 pounds; preferably a Sonoma
    County Liberty duck

1 yellow onion, quartered

1 carrot, roughly chopped

2 tomatoes, quartered

2 heads garlic, halved

1 bunch fresh sage

1 cup red wine

Pasta

3/4 cup flour

1 egg

1/2 teaspoon salt

Salt and freshly ground black pepper

6 *shiitake* mushroom caps, sliced

2 leeks, white and light green parts only,
    julienned

2 cloves garlic, chopped

1 bunch red chard, coarsely chopped

5 ounces sheep's milk ricotta, or
    goat cheese, crumbled

ROAST DUCK LASAGNE WITH GREENS AND SAGE

Serves 4. Wine recommendation: a spicy, oak-flavored Zinfandel

A Note on Procedure

The duck stock must be prepared at least 4 hours ahead.

Duck Stock

Preheat the oven to 425 degrees F.

Remove the breasts, legs and thighs from the duck. Reserve the legs and thighs for another meal or add them to the stock for richness and flavor. Set aside the breasts. Chop up the duck carcass and roast it in an ovenproof pan until it is lightly browned. Add the onion, carrot, tomatoes, garlic heads and sage stems and continue roasting until they are browned. (Reserve the sage leaves: The smaller leaves will be used in the pasta and the larger leaves will be used for garnish.) Leave the oven on. Place the browned bones and vegetables in a stockpot. Deglaze the roasting pan with the wine and add to the stockpot. Add cold water to cover and bring the mixture to a boil. Using a ladle, remove any scum that rises to the surface. Simmer for 2 hours and strain. Skim the fat from the surface. Pour the stock into a clean saucepan and reduce it by half to make a glaze. Set the glaze aside.

Pasta

Put the flour in a mixing bowl, make a well and add the egg and salt. Add the smaller sage leaves and combine the ingredients to form a dough. Add enough water to bring it together. Turn the dough onto a lightly floured board and knead approximately 10 minutes or until smooth. Wrap the dough in plastic and set it aside to rest for 30 minutes. When rested, run it through a pasta machine on the thinnest setting. Cut into 12 strips, each measuring 2 by 4 inches, flour lightly, cover and refrigerate.

Trim the duck breast and prick the skin side. Season with salt and pepper. In a hot ovenproof pan, place the breast skin side down and sear over medium-high heat on the stove top until it is lightly browned, approximately 4 minutes. Place the pan in the oven and roast until the skin is golden brown. Turn the breast once, cook it for 1 minute, remove it from the oven and keep it warm. Do not wash the pan, but pour off all but 1 tablespoon of excess fat.

One at a time, add the mushrooms, leeks, garlic and chard to the pan in which the duck breast was cooked, sautéing each before adding the next. If the pan needs more moisture, ladle in some of the duck glaze. Add 1 cup of the reserved glaze, cooking until the mixture is slightly thickened.

To assemble the lasagne, which is done separately for each serving, cook the pasta in batches: drop 4 pieces into a pot of boiling salted water, cook until the pasta is just al dente and drain. Place 1 piece of pasta on each serving plate. On it, layer slices of the duck breast, the sautéed vegetable mixture and the ricotta. While assembling, boil 4 more pieces of the pasta. When the pasta is cooked, create a second layer, using the duck slices, the sautéed vegetables and the ricotta. Boil the last 4 pieces of the pasta and lay one atop each lasagne. Garnish with the remaining sage. For a more elaborate presentation, garnish the dish with whole sage leaves fried in peanut oil.

FIG AND RASPBERRY GRATIN WITH PRALINE COOKIES

Serves 4. Wine recommendation: a tawny Port

Praline Cookies

1 cup sugar

1/3 cup water

1 cup toasted almonds or toasted, skinned hazelnuts

1 cup (2 sticks) unsalted butter, softened

3/4 cup light brown sugar, packed

1/2 teaspoon vanilla extract

1/2 teaspoon salt

2 cups flour

Fig and Raspberry Gratin

1 cup *crème fraîche*

1 basket fresh figs, preferably Adriatic

1 basket raspberries

1/4 to 1/3 cup brown sugar

Praline Cookies

Butter or lightly oil a baking sheet and set it aside.

To make the praline, stir the sugar and water together in a medium-sized saucepan until the sugar is wet. Heat the mixture at a low temperature until the sugar has dissolved and the liquid is clear. Raise the heat to high and wash down the sides of the pan with a brush dipped in cold water. Cook the mixture until it is golden brown, approximately 5 minutes. Do not stir. You can, however, swirl the pan carefully if the syrup is coloring unevenly. Take the pan off the heat and stir in the nuts with a wooden spoon. Return the pan to the heat just until the caramel liquefies, then pour it onto the prepared baking sheet. Set aside to cool, then coarsely chop the praline by hand or in a food processor. (Leftover praline can be wrapped in an airtight container and kept in the freezer.) *Makes 2 cups.*

In a mixing bowl, cream the butter and sugar until fluffy, then add the vanilla and salt. Stir in the flour and 3/4 cup chopped praline and mix until the ingredients are combined.

Refrigerate the dough for approximately 30 minutes. Preheat the oven to 375 degrees F. Roll out the dough approximately 1/4 inch thick and cut it into shapes or roll the dough into 2-inch-thick logs and cut them into 1/4-inch slices. Bake the cookies for 12 to 15 minutes on an ungreased baking sheet. Cool on a wire rack. *Makes approximately 4 dozen cookies.*

Fig and Raspberry Gratin

Preheat the broiler. Spread 1/4 cup of the *crème fraîche* on the bottom of each of 4 individual gratin dishes. Cut each fig into 4 or 5 slices and arrange them on top of the *crème fraîche*. Put 6 to 8 raspberries on top of the figs. Sprinkle 1 to 1 1/2 tablespoons brown sugar over the fruit. Place the gratin dishes under the hot broiler for 2 to 3 minutes until the sugar is melted and bubbly. Serve with the praline cookies.

John Ash and Company

When Fetzer Vineyards was ready to launch its ambitious food and wine education program, it turned to John Ash, described as "the king of the culinary mountain in Sonoma County" by the Wine Spectator magazine. To carry on the tradition of excellence at John Ash and Company, his own award-winning restaurant, Ash turned to his protégé, Jeff Madura. Ash's renowned style, which draws on French, Latin, and southwestern influences, requires skill and sensitivity, and he found both in Madura.

"Wine-country cooking is really about showing people the wide variety of regional products available and educating the public about what a special place the region is," Madura says. "My personal approach to food is to use the freshest ingredients we can find in the wine country and to showcase them in the simplest preparation possible."

The restaurant itself, with its French windows that invite in the surrounding landscape and a trellised patio that gives a view of nearby vineyards and distant mountains, is another kind of showcase for the wine country. Set in a fifty acre vineyard, off a deserted country road, it shares its entrancing setting with the Vintners Inn, a charming European-style hotel. The elegant, understated service encourages diners to settle in and explore a menu that ranges from a terrine of roasted Petaluma duck to a mixed seafood platter featuring the day's catch from the California coast.

"Living in this area has really shaped me," Madura says, "not only as a chef but also as a consumer, making me aware of what it takes to raise the products: love, hard work, and dealing with Mother Nature."

CRAB CAKES WITH CABBAGE SLAW AND BLOOD ORANGE MAYONNAISE

Serves 4. Wine recommendation: a tart Sauvignon Blanc or crisp Chardonnay

Cabbage Slaw

1 cup thinly sliced red cabbage

1 cup thinly sliced green cabbage

1/4 cup seeded and thinly sliced bell
  red pepper

1 cup thinly sliced carrot

1/4 cup raspberry vinegar

1/8 cup extra virgin olive oil

1/2 teaspoon minced garlic

1 teaspoon Dijon mustard

Kosher salt and freshly ground black
  pepper, to taste

Blood Orange Mayonnaise

1 whole egg

2 egg yolks

1/2 teaspoon mustard powder mixed
  with 1/4 teaspoon cold water

1/2 cup minced green onions

3 tablespoons red wine vinegar

2 blood oranges, peeled, seeded and
  chopped, juice reserved

1/2 teaspoon kosher salt

1/2 teaspoon freshly ground white pepper

1 1/4 cups peanut oil

Crab Cakes

1 pound Dungeness crabmeat

1/2 cup fresh dry bread crumbs or *Panko**

1 large egg, beaten

5 tablespoons mayonnaise

1 tablespoon minced parsley

5 tablespoons minced green onions

2 teaspoons white wine Worcestershire
  sauce

2 teaspoons mustard powder mixed
  with 1 teaspoon cold water

1/2 teaspoon salt

1/4 teaspoon freshly ground white pepper

6 to 8 drops Tabasco sauce (optional)

Clarified butter or light olive oil

1 bunch spinach, cleaned

**Panko* is a flaked Japanese bread crumb
that can be found in Asian markets.

Cabbage Slaw

Combine the cabbages, red pepper and carrot in a bowl. In a separate bowl, make the dressing by combining the vinegar, olive oil, garlic, mustard, salt and pepper. Toss the vegetables with the dressing. Let the mixture stand for 10 minutes, tossing it occasionally. Set aside.

Blood Orange Mayonnaise

Have all the ingredients at room temperature. Place the egg, egg yolks, mustard, green onions, vinegar, blood orange and reserved juice, and salt and pepper in a food processor and process until the mixture is pale yellow and foamy. Add a tablespoon of the oil and mix until it is absorbed. With the processor running, continue to add the oil in a very slow stream until it has all been incorporated. Taste the mayonnaise and adjust the seasoning if needed.

Store, tightly covered, in the refrigerator. This mayonnaise, which is sufficiently liquid to be used in a squeeze bottle, will keep for approximately a week. *Makes 1 3/4 cups.*

Crab Cakes

Pick over the crabmeat carefully to remove any bits of shell or cartilage. In a mixing bowl, combine the bread crumbs, egg, mayonnaise, parsley, green onions, Worcestershire sauce, mustard, salt and pepper and Tabasco, if using, with the crabmeat, but do not overmix. The mixture should have some definite texture. Form into 12 small cakes and sauté them in a large heavy-bottomed pan over medium-high heat in clarified butter or light olive oil until they are lightly browned on both sides, approximately 3 minutes per side.

Immediately before serving, wilt the spinach briefly in a hot sauté pan and season with salt and pepper. To serve, place 3 cakes on a bed of lightly wilted spinach leaves, arrange the cabbage slaw alongside and garnish with a dollop of blood orange mayonnaise.

SQUAB BRAISED IN CIDER

4 squab

Salt and freshly ground black pepper

1/4 cup olive oil, rendered bacon fat
or rendered duck fat

2 cups sliced yellow onion

4 cloves garlic, slivered

3 shallots, slivered

3 cups (1/4 head) finely shredded
red cabbage

4 tart apples, peeled and cut into 1/4-inch
wedges (approximately 4 cups)

1/2 cup chicken stock

1 cup dry white wine

3 cups natural apple cider

3 tablespoons raspberry or black
currant vinegar

2/3 cup whole, peeled fresh chestnuts
or unsweetened canned chestnuts,
drained

1 tablespoon chopped fresh rosemary
or 1 1/2 teaspoons dried rosemary

2 tablespoons unsalted butter

1/2 tart apple, thinly sliced

Fresh rosemary sprigs, for garnish

Serves 4. Wine recommendation: an oak-flavored Chardonnay with apple undertones

Preheat the oven to 400 degrees F.

Season the squab with salt and pepper. In an ovenproof pan, heat 2 tablespoons of the oil over a medium-high heat and quickly brown the squab, 2 at a time; set them aside. Wipe out the pan with a paper towel to remove burned bits if necessary. Add the remaining 2 tablespoons of oil and sauté the onion, garlic and shallots until they are lightly colored, approximately 7 minutes. Add the cabbage, apples, stock, wine, cider and vinegar and bring the mixture to a boil. Remove the pan from the heat.

Using a slotted utensil, remove 2 cups of the vegetables from the pan, drain them well and loosely stuff them into the squab cavities. Transfer the remaining vegetables and liquid to a roasting pan large enough to accommodate all of the ingredients. Arrange the squab on top of the vegetable mixture and add the chestnuts and the rosemary. Cover tightly and bake in the oven until the squab is just cooked (the juices should run light pink when the thigh joint is pierced), approximately 25 minutes.

Remove the squab and keep them warm. Strain the vegetables and set them aside. Pour the cooking liquid into a saucepan and reduce it over high heat to a thin sauce. Taste and adjust the seasoning.

Melt the butter in a small pan and quickly sauté the apple slices over medium heat, turning once, until they soften and turn golden brown.

To serve, arrange the vegetables and squab on warm plates and garnish with sautéed apple slices and sprigs of rosemary.

ALMOND ORANGE TART WITH GINGER CRÈME ANGLAISE

Makes one 9-inch tart; serves 8. Wine recommendation: a late-harvest Riesling or late-harvest Sauvignon Blanc

Tart Shell

In a mixing bowl, combine the flour, butter and vanilla until the dough resembles coarse oatmeal. If it is too dry, add drops of ice water. Gather the dough into a ball, cover with plastic and chill it for at least 30 minutes.

Preheat the oven to 350 degrees F. Roll out the dough to fit a 9-inch, removable-bottom tart pan. Prick the dough well and bake it for 6 to 8 minutes until the crust is set and very lightly browned. Let cool. Leave the oven on.

Filling

Heat the sugar and cream in a saucepan over medium heat until it just simmers and the mixture becomes translucent. Stir in the zest, vanilla, salt and liqueur.

Line the tart shell with an even layer of almonds and pour the cream mixture over them. Place the tart on a baking sheet and bake it for 30 to 35 minutes until lightly browned on top. (The filling will bubble up as it bakes.) Let the tart cool; do not refrigerate it.

While the tart is baking, prepare the ginger *crème anglaise*.

Ginger Crème Anglaise

Place the ginger, 1/4 cup of the sugar and the water in a medium saucepan and simmer over moderate heat for approximately 10 minutes. The syrup should be thick but not brown. Set the syrup aside, off the heat, for 30 minutes to allow the flavor to develop. Return the pan to the heat, add the cream and vanilla extract and bring the mixture just to a simmer.

In a bowl, beat the egg yolks with the remaining 1/4 cup sugar. Stir in the hot cream mixture slowly to avoid scrambling the eggs. Return the custard mixture to the saucepan and cook over moderate heat until the sauce begins to thicken; it should register 180 degrees F on a candy thermometer. Immediately strain the custard and refrigerate it, covered. *Makes 3 cups.*

Serve the tart warm or at room tempurature. Garnish with fresh berries and serve it with ginger *crème anglaise*.

Tart Shell
1 cup flour
1/2 cup unsalted butter, chilled and
    diced small
1 teaspoon vanilla
1 to 2 tablespoons ice water, if needed

Filling
3/4 cup sugar
3/4 cup heavy cream
1 tablespoon minced orange zest
1/2 teaspoon vanilla extract
Big pinch of salt
2 tablespoons Grand Marnier liqueur
    or other orange-flavored liqueur
2 cups almonds, sliced

Fresh berries, for garnish

Ginger Crème Anglaise
1/4 cup peeled and roughly chopped
    fresh ginger*
1/2 cup sugar
1/4 cup water
2 cups light cream
1 teaspoon vanilla extract
6 egg yolks

*Even though it is to be strained out of the custard, the ginger should be peeled because the skin is often bitter.

Samba Java

It's hard to miss Samba Java as you stroll the plaza in central Healdsburg—it's the place with the galvanized tin table tops, brightly painted wood chairs, and strings of colorful lights that make you think of someplace tropical. Step inside, past the arching windows, and you're in a different world. Sit down at a table, and you'll be given a menu with such cross-cultural dishes as Thai gingered carrot soup, fried calamari with chile jam, grilled black bean spareribs, and peppered beef top round.

"At eighteen, I left home for France and was exposed to the incredible new world of food as culture," recalls the chef, Colleen McGlynn. Thereafter, she alternated stints overseas with cooking jobs in the United States, including four years at Stars in San Francisco. The result is what McGlynn calls "California eclectic" or "New World" cooking: a style that is "faithful to classical techniques and methodologies and open to cuisines experienced while traveling."

The menu changes daily, depending on what's available—and whether someone on the kitchen staff has just returned from abroad. "Wine-country cooking, while not so different from that in some San Francisco restaurants, is perhaps more vibrant," McGlynn says. "It's the close connection to the food source. Our menus directly reflect the farmers' input and the bounty of their crops."

One of the best times of year to visit Samba Java is in March. To celebrate the end of winter, McGlynn hosts a merry, colorful celebration "Carnival-Caribe," when diners can sample a variety of ethnic dishes from New Orleans, Brazil, and the Caribbean such as fried pork, black beans, and plantains.

SPICY COCONUT AND PUMPKIN SOUP

Serves 8. Wine recommendation: a dry, barrel-fermented Gewürztraminer

2 cans (14 ounces each) coconut milk

2 cans water

1 small pumpkin, peeled, seeded and
    sliced into crescents 1/4 inch thick
    and 1 inch long

3 stalks fresh lemongrass, cut diagonally,
    1/4 inch thick

6 slices fresh *galangal*,* each the size of
    a quarter (or 3 slices fresh ginger)

6 Thai chiles (or substitute *serrano* chiles)

6 cloves garlic, peeled and roughly chopped

6 *serrano* chiles, seeded and roughly
    chopped

Juice of 2 limes

1/4 cup sugar

1/2 cup fish sauce

1 bunch basil leaves, cut into fine strips

1/2 pound snow peas, ends and
    strings removed

1/2 pound oyster mushrooms, woody
    stems removed

*Galangal can be found in Asian markets frozen, dried or as a powder labeled "*laos* powder." Be aware that it is not really interchangeable with ginger, which lacks its citruslike, perfume qualities.

In a medium soup pot, bring to a boil the coconut milk, water, pumpkin (if pumpkin is not available, a hard squash such as butternut may be substituted but should be added later in the cooking), lemongrass, *galangal* and the Thai chiles. Simmer the mixture for 10 minutes.

Meanwhile, in a mortar, mash together the garlic, *serrano* chiles, lime juice, sugar and fish sauce with a pestle until the mixture becomes a smooth sauce. (Using a food processor will result in a slightly different viscosity, but no impairment in taste.) Add the sauce to the soup. (If using squash instead of pumpkin, add to the soup at this point.) Simmer the soup for 15 to 20 minutes, or until the pumpkin is tender. Add the basil, snow peas and mushrooms. Continue simmering until all the ingredients are heated through and serve immediately.

8 pounds pork spareribs, approximately
    2 sides
Kosher salt
1/2 cup granulated sugar
4 bay leaves
2 tablespoons red-pepper flakes
1 piece ginger, 3 inches long (approximately
    2 ounces), peeled
4 cloves garlic, peeled
6 *serrano* chiles, seeded
1 bunch cilantro, roughly chopped
1/2 cup rice vinegar
1/4 cup sesame oil
1/4 cup soy sauce
3/4 cup vegetable oil
1/4 cup brown sugar
3/4 cup Chinese fermented black
    beans, rinsed

Confetti Slaw
Half of a red cabbage, thinly sliced
Half of a white cabbage, thinly sliced
2 teaspoons kosher salt
1 small napa cabbage, thinly sliced
2 carrots, grated
1 bunch cilantro, chopped
1/2 cup rice vinegar
1/4 cup vegetable oil
1 tablespoon sugar
1 jalapeño pepper, seeded and
    finely chopped
1/2 cup toasted, chopped peanuts
Salt and freshly ground black pepper,
    to taste

Fried Plantains
6 large green plantains
Vegetable oil, for frying
1 1/2 cups water mixed with 4 teaspoons
    kosher salt
2 limes
Red-pepper flakes

CHINESE BLACK BEAN SPARERIBS
WITH CONFETTI SLAW AND FRIED PLANTAINS

Serves 8. Wine recommendation: a fruity Zinfandel or smoky, black cherry Pinot Noir

A Note on Procedure
You will need to start a day ahead to soak the ribs overnight.

Place the spareribs in a large pan and cover with cold water. Add enough kosher salt to make the water taste salty (like sea water) and 1/4 cup of the granulated sugar. Refrigerate the mixture overnight.

Preheat the oven to 325 degrees F. Drain off the brine and place the ribs in a roasting pan, covering them again with cold water. Remove the ribs temporarily. Add enough salt to the water to make it taste like sea water, then add the remaining sugar, the bay leaves and the red-pepper flakes. Put the ribs back in, cover the pan and bake in the oven for 2 1/2 to 3 hours. Adjust the heat so that the water is never above a gentle simmer. Don't be nervous if it seems to take forever; braising takes time.

While the ribs are cooking, prepare the marinade. In a food processor, combine the ginger, garlic, chiles and cilantro and pulse until the ingredients are roughly chopped. Add the vinegar, sesame oil, soy sauce, vegetable oil and brown sugar. Pulse for a few seconds more. Add the black beans. Pulse for 2 seconds. Set aside.

When the meat feels tender and bones somewhat loose, remove the pan from the oven. (This is your call. Some people like to chew ribs; others are of the fall-off-the-bone sort.) Slather the ribs with half of the marinade.

Confetti Slaw
In a colander, toss the red and white cabbage with the kosher salt. Set the cabbage aside to soften. After approximately 15 minutes, squeeze out any liquid. In a medium bowl, combine the cabbages, the carrots and the cilantro.

In a small saucepan, boil the vinegar, oil, sugar and jalapeño together for 1 minute. Set the mixture aside to cool. Just before serving, drain the excess liquid from the vegetables, toss them with the dressing, add the peanuts and adjust the seasoning with salt and pepper. Refrigerate any extra slaw. *Makes 12 cups.*

Fried Plantains
Peel and cut the plantains into 1–inch slices. Heat approximately 2 inches of oil in a heavy skillet over medium heat. Add the plantains in batches, cooking each side for 2 minutes and turning once, until they are tender but not crusty. Remove them from the oil. Lay each slice of plantain between sheets of waxed paper and flatten it to approximately 1/4 inch thick. Dip the slices into the salted water, return them to the skillet and fry them over high heat until golden. Drain, squeeze lime juice over them and sprinkle on red-pepper flakes.

When you are ready to grill, let the coals attain a fine white ash covering and then rake them out. Make sure that your grill rack is hot and clean. Place the ribs on the rack, which should be at least 6 inches from the coals. The point of the grilling is to get some smoke flavor, caramelize the sugar and meld the flavors; only make a gentle fire, or you'll have flare-ups. Cook the ribs on one side for a few minutes, turn, add some more marinade and continue cooking until you have a glistening surface. Arrange the ribs on a platter and serve with the confetti slaw and fried plantains.

GINGER CRÈME BRÛLÉE

Serves 6. Wine recommendation: a late-harvest Riesling

3 egg yolks
1 whole egg
1/3 cup granulated sugar
3/4 cup whole milk
1 1/3 cups heavy cream
1/2 ounce peeled and finely chopped
    fresh ginger (a knob approximately
    the size of your thumb)
3 tablespoons superfine sugar

Preheat the oven to 300 degrees F.

In a medium bowl, whisk together the yolks, whole egg and granulated sugar. Set the mixture aside. In a medium saucepan, combine the milk, cream and ginger. Heat the mixture over moderate heat until it begins to climb up the sides of the pan. Whisk a small amount of the hot milk into the eggs to temper them, then whisk in the rest. Strain the mixture into a pitcher, pressing down on the ginger to extract the flavor. (The custard can be prepared ahead to this point and refrigerated, but baking time will need to be increased because the custard will be chilled.)

Pour the custard into six 4–ounce ramekins, filling them to within 1/4 inch of the top. Place the ramekins in a pan that is large enough to hold them all without touching. Place the pan on the middle shelf of the oven, then fill the pan with hot water to reach halfway up the sides of the ramekins. Cover with foil and bake the custards for 45 to 50 minutes or until all but a small, round 1-inch spot in the center is set. Remove the ramekins from the pan and let them cool on a rack.

To serve, preheat the broiler. Sprinkle a layer of superfine sugar over the custard to cover the surface and set the ramekins in a pan of ice (to prevent the custard from heating up). Place the pan under the broiler until the sugar is caramelized. Serve immediately.

Bistro Ralph

Despite a French-inflected culinary pedigree that includes Le Cordon Bleu, Le Cirque in New York, and the Auberge du Soleil in the Napa Valley, Ralph Tingle yearned for a restaurant where the cuisine was as unpretentious as it was fresh. "I wanted a place that served food I would enjoy eating everyday," he says. When a restaurant space opened just off the main square of the small Sonoma town of Healdsburg, Tingle jumped. "Without a penny raised or a lease, I took the big leap!"

Bistro Ralph opened in the summer of 1992 with a seasonal menu updated each week. Since then, the menu has broadened to include more meats and fowl, but Tingle's insistence on fresh local ingredients is unwavering. "You can see me at the farmers' market in Healdsburg every Tuesday and Saturday," he says. "We even buy our flowers there." Tingle also insists on local wine. So local, in fact, that everything on the wine list at Bistro Ralph comes from the surrounding Healdsburg appellation.

The interior of the bistro is more French modern than California traditional, with a distressed steel doorway leading into the sleek, sophisticated bar and restaurant. The hospitality, though, is more Mediterranean. A plate of focaccine *accented with fennel seeds arrives at the table soon after you do, and you'll be hard pressed to resist it while your meal is being prepared in the kitchen.*

"Wine-country cuisine comes from the garden," Tingle feels. "Not too much fuss, just flavors, textures, and sensibility. At Bistro Ralph, we're trying to deliver a good, comfortable meal that is rewarding in its simplicity."

ANISE-FLAVORED FOCACCINE

1 1/2 to 2 cups water

1 tablespoon active dry yeast
  (one 1/4-ounce package)

5 1/2 cups organic, unbleached bread flour

Salt and freshly ground black pepper

6 tablespoons virgin olive oil

2 tablespoons toasted fennel seed

2 tablespoons Pernod

1 egg beaten with 2 tablespoons water,
  for egg wash

Makes 5 dozen bite-sized rolls; serves 8 to 10. Wine recommendation: a barrel-fermented Sauvignon Blanc

Warm 1 cup of the water to 150 degrees F (perceptibly warm, but not hot), pour into a small bowl and dissolve the yeast in it. In the bowl of an electric mixer, mix the flour, salt and pepper, the yeast mixture, 2 tablespoons of the olive oil, the fennel seeds and the Pernod. Add enough of the remaining water to form a dough.

Turn the dough out onto a floured board and knead it by hand for 10 minutes, until it is soft and satiny, or for 8 minutes in a mixer with a dough hook.

Set the dough aside, covered and in a warm place, to rise for 1 hour.

Preheat the oven to 500 degrees F. Punch the dough down, then using your palms, roll the dough into 1-inch balls. Brush the balls with the egg wash and bake 8 to 12 minutes until the tops turn golden brown.

Let the *focaccine* cool. When you are ready to serve them, heat the remaining 4 tablespoons olive oil in a sauté pan over medium heat and toss the rolls briefly in the oil. Sprinkle with some salt. Serve immediately.

BRAISED CHILEAN SEA BASS

8- to 12-inch piece fresh peeled ginger

1/2 cup sesame seeds, preferably a mixture
   of black and white

4 fillets (7 ounces each) fresh, boneless
   Chilean sea bass

Salt and freshly ground black pepper

3 tablespoons unsalted butter

3 cups fresh carrot juice, homemade or
   commercial

Cilantro sprigs, for garnish

Serves 4. Wine recommendation: a full-bodied, buttery, barrel-fermented Chardonnay

Roughly chop the peeled ginger in a food processor. Place the pulp in a thin kitchen towel and squeeze the juice into a small bowl. Set aside. Lightly toast the sesame seeds in a dry sauté pan over medium heat for 3 to 4 minutes, stirring often. Set aside to cool.

Preheat the oven to 450 degrees F.

Season the fish with salt and pepper on both sides, then dip one side of each piece in the sesame seeds.

In an ovenproof sauté pan with a metal handle, melt 1 tablespoon of the butter over medium heat, tilting the pan to coat the bottom with the butter. Place the fish in the pan, coated side up, without allowing the pieces to touch. Pour in the carrot and ginger juices, bring to a simmer and place the pan in the oven for 9 to 10 minutes.

Remove the pan from the oven and transfer the fish directly onto warm plates or into shallow bowls. Keep the fish warm. Reduce the juice over high heat until 1 1/2 cups remain. The juice will appear very "broken" and curdled. Whisk in the remaining 2 tablespoons butter, remove from the heat and season with salt and pepper to taste. If the sauce still looks "broken," emulsify it in a blender. Pour the sauce around the fish, garnish with the cilantro and serve immediately.

CHOCOLATE PÂTÉ

4 ounces high-quality bittersweet chocolate

1 cup (2 sticks) unsalted butter

1/4 cup sugar, plus 1 tablespoon sugar
    for sweetening the cream

1 1/2 tablespoons cocoa

3 egg yolks

2 egg whites

1/2 cup heavy cream

1 to 2 cups whipped cream

Serves 8 to 10. Wine recommendation: a full-bodied, fruity, dry Zinfandel

Chop the chocolate into small pieces to help it melt evenly. Place the pieces in a large mixing bowl set over simmering water. Add the butter, the 1/4 cup of sugar and the cocoa and let these ingredients melt with the chocolate, stirring occasionally. Do not overheat or the chocolate will separate.

Once the chocolate has melted, remove the bowl from the heat and let the mixture cool almost to room temperature, then beat in the egg yolks.

In a bowl, whip the egg whites, being careful not to overwhip. In a separate bowl, whip the cream, sweetening it to taste with the remaining sugar, also being careful not to overwhip. Fold the cream and then the egg whites into the chocolate mixture.

Line a narrow, rectangular pâté mold or loaf pan (3 by 3 by 8 inches) with plastic wrap, pour in the mixture, cover loosely with plastic wrap and refrigerate. The pâté will take approximately 2 hours to set. Unmold the pâté, slice it and serve with whipped cream.

Downtown Bakery and Creamery

One night over dinner, Kathleen Stewart and Lindsey Shere got to talking. Both were living in rural northern Sonoma County and working at Chez Panisse in urban Berkeley. They were tired of the commute and Sonoma's lack of the breads, desserts, and coffee they found in the city. They decided to do something about it.

Healdsburg residents (and savvy visitors) have been getting their pastry and hanging out at the Downtown Bakery and Creamery ever since. "Our idea was to have a very small place we could run ourselves," Stewart recalls. "But very soon we saw that the bakery had a life of its own. People come every morning with their own coffee mugs and sit with their friends outside." Those who sit inside the old-time bakery are served on an eclectic assortment of china that Shere and Stewart picked up at antique stores and flea markets.

Shere (who still makes pastries at Chez Panisse during the week) and Stewart present the fruits, nuts, and berries from the surrounding area in different ways. The bakery produces everything from old-fashioned sticky buns, scones, and fresh fruit tarts to breads ranging from sourdough French to Italian focaccia. A flaky pastry crust is used for fresh strawberry and rhubarb pies, and the croissant dough used in the pecan twists takes four days to make. There are six flavors of shortbread cookies alone.

True to its name, the Downtown Bakery and Creamery makes rich ice creams and fruity sorbets. "We wanted to bring people a kind of baking and ice cream making that was available in only a few restaurants in our area," Stewart says, "in a place they would feel at home."

APPLE POLENTA TART

Serves 8

Pastry
1/2 cup sugar
6 tablespoons plus 1 teaspoon unsalted
　butter
2 egg yolks
1 cup flour
1/3 cup plus 3 tablespoons cornmeal or
　medium-fine polenta
1/2 teaspoon salt

Filling
2 pounds apples (preferably McIntosh,
　Sierra Beauty or Empire)
1 teaspoon flour
2 tablespoons sugar, or more, to taste
1 egg yolk
1/2 tablespoon heavy cream
A few tablespoons coarse crystal sugar,
　for topping

Pastry

Preheat the oven to 375 degrees F.

In the bowl of an electric mixer, cream the sugar and butter. Add the egg yolks and beat until the mixture is light. In a separate bowl, combine the flour, the 1/3 cup cornmeal and salt. Add to the egg mixture and beat just until the ingredients hold together. Mixture will resemble pea-sized cornmeal. Push dough together and form into 2 disks, one slightly larger than the other. Refrigerate the dough for 1 hour. Roll out the larger disk between 2 sheets of plastic wrap to fit into a 9-inch tart pan. Remove the top sheet of plastic, invert the pastry into the pan, peel off the second sheet of plastic and cut off any excess pastry. Refrigerate the shell for 1 hour to let the dough relax.

Ten minutes before you plan to bake the pastry, preheat the oven to 375 degrees F. Partially bake the shell until it is a light golden brown, 12 to 15 minutes. Cool slightly and sprinkle the 3 tablespoons cornmeal over the bottom of the shell. Leave the oven on.

Filling

Core, peel and quarter the apples, then slice them 1/4 inch thick. Mix the flour and sugar in a large bowl and toss the apples in the mixture.

Fill the shell with the prepared apples. Roll out the smaller disk of dough and lay it over the apples. Press it to the edge of the dish all around the pan. Lightly beat the egg yolk with the cream and brush the top of the tart with the mixture. Sprinkle the top with the coarse sugar and bake until golden brown and the apples are done, approximately 45 to 55 minutes. If the crust is browning too quickly and the apples are not yet fully cooked, reduce the oven temperature to 325 degrees F.

The pastry recipe is by courtesy of Carol Field.

BLUEBERRY SCONES

Makes 12 to 14 scones

3 cups flour
3 tablespoons sugar
1 tablespoon baking powder
1/2 teaspoon baking soda
3/4 teaspoon salt
3/4 cup (1 1/2 sticks) unsalted butter,
　cold and cut into small pieces
1 cup fresh blueberries, or frozen,
　then thawed to room temperature
　and drained
1 egg
1 cup buttermilk
2 tablespoons milk

Preheat the oven to 375 degrees F.

In a mixing bowl, combine the flour, 2 tablespoons of the sugar, baking powder, baking soda and salt. With a pastry knife or your fingers, blend the butter with the dry ingredients until the mixture has the consistency of cornmeal. Add the blueberries.

Break the egg into a small bowl and mix it lightly with a fork. Add the buttermilk to the egg and again mix lightly. Add this mixture to the dry ingredients and mix only until the dough comes together. Do not overmix or the scones will be tough.

Turn the dough out onto a lightly floured surface and pat or roll it out into a rectangle 1 inch thick. Cut into rounds with a 2-inch circular cutter. Place the scones on a nonstick baking sheet or line the sheet with baking parchment. Brush the tops with milk and sprinkle on the remaining tablespoon of sugar. Bake the scones for 20 to 24 minutes until they are browned and puffy. Cool on a wire rack.

Madrona Manor

Drive up to Madrona Manor and you enter a gracious world of well-groomed lawns, lush gardens, and silver-green vineyards surrounding a grand, three-story gabled Victorian mansion. The mood continues inside, where the intimate dining rooms have tall windows draped in curtains, gilt-edged mirrors, and ornate chandeliers. The grandeur of the inn and the fast-rising reputation of its chef, Todd Muir, are a magnet for chefs from around the world who come to eat, share ideas, and cook for Madrona Manor diners.

Muir's parents opened Madrona Manor, a country inn built in 1881 on the outskirts of Healdsburg, in 1982 with the help of their daughter and three sons. Training at the California Culinary Academy and two years under Alice Waters at Chez Panisse was all that Todd needed to set up the kitchen at Madrona Manor, and his cooking quickly earned it national acclaim.

"The Academy taught me how to cook," Muir says. "Alice taught me what to cook." He cautions against the idea that California cuisine, which Waters helped pioneer, is just "indigenous foodstuffs served on sparse plates." Rather, it encompasses the cuisines of all the peoples that give California its rich ethnic diversity.

"Color is extremely important," Muir emphasizes, and a plate from his kitchen is a delight to the eye. Still, it is flavor that reigns supreme, and if Muir can't find a smoked salmon or peppery chorizo with the depth and drama he requires, he smokes it or makes it himself.

DUCK CONFIT AGNOLOTTI WITH FALL SQUASH SAUCE AND LEMON CREAM

Serves 8. Wine recommendation: a rich Chardonnay or light Pinot Noir

A Note on Procedure
The confit needs to be made at least a day in advance.

Duck Confit
In a small bowl, mix the bay leaves, thyme and pepper with the salt. Place the duck legs in a glass dish large enough to fit comfortably. Sprinkle the salt mixture over the duck legs and refrigerate them overnight. The following day, rinse the duck legs off under running water. Heat the duck fat in a large pan over medium-high heat until it is simmering. Poach the legs in the fat until the meat comes off the bone, approximately 1 hour. Remove the duck legs from the pan of fat and let them cool. Take all of the meat off the legs, discarding the skin and bones.

Duck Filling
Shred the duck *confit* in a mixer, using the paddle attachment. Add the bread crumbs, egg and herbs. If necessary, season to taste with salt and pepper; it may be salty enough.

Agnolotti Dough
Mix the flour, eggs, olive oil and salt together in a food processor. Turn the dough out onto a floured surface and knead it by hand for a few minutes. Cover the dough with plastic wrap and let it rest for 30 minutes.

Divide the dough in half. Roll out the dough slightly with a rolling pin. Then, progressing to the thinnest setting (#7) on a pasta machine, roll the dough into thin sheets. Cover the sheets with plastic wrap as you work to prevent them from drying out.

To assemble the *agnolotti*, cut out 12 circles of pasta from each sheet with a 4-inch round cutter. Brush each circle lightly with water and place 1 teaspoon of the duck filling in the center and fold the pasta over to enclose the filling in a half moon. Press the edge down firmly. *Makes 24 agnolotti.*

Fall Squash Sauce
Preheat the oven to 350 degrees F.

Cut the acorn squash in half, scoop out the seeds and place the squash cut side down on a baking sheet lined with parchment paper. Bake the squash for 30 to 40 minutes, or until it is soft to the touch. Turn the squash over and set it aside to cool. Remove the skin.

In a sauté pan, cook the onion in the butter over medium heat for 3 minutes. Add the squash and the carrot. Cover the vegetables with the stock and simmer for 15 minutes. When the carrot is soft, pass the mixture through a food mill. Season with salt and pepper.

Lemon Cream
Place the cream cheese in a small bowl and thin out with 2 tablespoons of the milk. Add the lemon juice and the zest. Season with the sugar and the salt. Thin the sauce with more milk if necessary and pour into a squeeze bottle.

Poach the *agnolotti* in a large pot of boiling water for 5 minutes and drain.

To serve, place 3 tablespoons of fall squash sauce on each of 8 plates. Arrange 3 *agnolotti* on each plate and decorate the sauce on each plate with 3 swirls of lemon cream.

Duck Confit

8 bay leaves, crumbled
1 tablespoon thyme leaves
1 tablespoon cracked black peppercorns
2 tablespoons rock salt
4 duck legs
1 quart duck fat or 2 pounds lard

Duck Filling

1 recipe duck confit
1/2 cup fresh white bread crumbs
1 egg
3 tablespoons mixed fresh or dried herbs
    (such as rosemary, thyme, oregano or
    herbes de Provence), chopped
Salt and freshly ground black pepper,
    to taste

Agnolotti Dough

2 cups flour
3 eggs
2 tablespoons cold-pressed olive oil
1 teaspoon salt

Fall Squash Sauce

1 acorn squash
Half a yellow onion, coarsely chopped
2 tablespoons unsalted butter
Half a carrot, finely chopped
Homemade chicken stock, to cover
    (1 1/2 to 2 cups)
Salt and freshly ground pepper, to taste

Lemon Cream

1/4 cup cream cheese, softened
2 or 3 tablespoons milk
Juice from 1/2 lemon
1 teaspoon lemon zest, minced
Sugar and salt, to taste

Black Bean Purée
2 cups black beans

9 cups chicken stock, preferably homemade

Half an onion, chopped

1 tablespoon minced garlic

Salt and freshly ground black pepper

Marinade
1/2 cup white wine

1 lemon, thinly sliced

1/2 cup olive oil

1 tablespoon chopped mixed fresh herbs,
    including thyme, rosemary, oregano
    and parsley

2 tablespoons cracked black pepper

8 veal loin steaks (5 ounces each),
    trimmed of all fat and silverskin

Medley of Peppers
2 Anaheim chiles, seeded and sliced
    into rings

4 red cherry peppers, cut in half,
    seeds removed

1 yellow pepper, seeded and
    cut into rings

Half a green bell pepper, finely julienned

Half a red bell pepper, finely julienned

Half an orange bell pepper, finely julienned

1 tablespoon extra virgin olive oil

1 tablespoon water

Pinch of cumin

Salt and freshly ground pepper, to taste

Corn Salsa
12 sun-dried tomatoes, coarsely chopped

Half a red onion, minced

1 tablespoon finely sliced green onions

1 cup cooked corn kernels

1/2 cup extra virgin olive oil

Lemon juice, to taste

Salt and freshly ground pepper, to taste

VEAL LOIN WITH A MEDLEY OF PEPPERS, BLACK BEAN PURÉE AND CORN SALSA

Serves 8. Wine recommendation: a California Rhône-style wine

A Note on Procedure
Cook the beans and marinate the veal 2 hours ahead.

Black Bean Purée
Cook the beans in a large pot with 8 cups of the stock, the onion and garlic for 2 hours, or until they are tender. Purée the mixture in a food processor, adding the remaining cup of stock if needed: The purée should be neither too thick nor too thin. Season to taste with salt and pepper. Spoon the purée into a pastry bag fitted with a fluted tip.

Marinade
To make the marinade, in a large nonreactive bowl, combine the wine, lemon slices, oil, herbs and pepper. Place the veal in the marinade and marinate for 2 hours in the refrigerator.

Medley of Peppers
In a saucepan over medium-high heat, sauté the peppers in the oil for 1 to 2 minutes. Add the water, cover, lower the heat and cook until the peppers are softened, approximately 5 minutes. Season with the cumin, salt and pepper. Keep warm.

Corn Salsa
In a bowl, mix thoroughly the tomatoes, onions, corn and olive oil. Season with the lemon juice, salt and pepper.

When you are ready to cook the veal, prepare a mesquite-fired grill. Grill the meat to the desired doneness, approximately 4 to 6 minutes on each side.

To serve, place a veal steak in the center of each of 4 large plates. Spoon some corn salsa over the veal. Place the pepper medley on one side of the veal and pipe the black bean purée on the other side.

2 tablespoons unsalted butter

2 tablespoons flour

1 cup milk

1/4 cup sugar

1/4 cup apricot brandy

1/2 cup (4 ounces) dried apricots,
   reconstituted in hot water until
   soft, then coarsely chopped

1/2 cup plus 2 tablespoons apricot jam

1/2 teaspoon vanilla extract

Pinch of salt

4 egg yolks, beaten

6 egg whites

12 sheets phyllo dough

1/2 cup melted butter, white solids
   removed

1/2 cup raspberry jam

1/2 cup blackberry jam

1/2 cup kiwi jam

1/2 cup strawberry jam

APRICOT SOUFFLÉS IN PHYLLO PASTRY ON A PALETTE OF FRUIT SAUCES

Serves 8. Wine recommendation: a late-harvest Gewürztraminer

A Note on Procedure

Prepare the soufflé mixture a day ahead.

Melt the butter over medium heat in a 2-quart, heavy-bottomed saucepan. Add the flour and cook, stirring, for a minute or two. Add the milk, the sugar and the brandy. Whisk for approximately 3 minutes until fairly thick, adding more milk if it is too thick. Add the apricots, the 2 tablespoons of apricot jam, vanilla and salt and cook for a minute or two longer. Let the mixture cool and add the yolks. In a separate bowl, whip the egg whites to soft peaks and gently fold them into the apricot mixture.

Grease or spray eight 4-ounce ramekins with nonstick vegetable spray. Spoon the soufflé mixture into the ramekins and freeze until the mixture is firm, approximately 6 hours or overnight.

Just before the soufflés are to be served, heat the oven to 375 degrees F. Cut one sheet of phyllo dough in half; cover the rest with a damp towel. Brush the halves with clarified butter on one side. Top each buttered sheet with a second half-sheet of phyllo dough set at an angle and brush the top with clarified butter. Cut another sheet of phyllo in half and brush the halves with clarified butter. Set the sheet on top of the second layer of phyllo at a different angle, so you have a star formation. Remove 2 frozen soufflés from their ramekins, using a knife to loosen the edges. Place each soufflé upright in the middle of a prepared sheet of phyllo. Gather up the corners of the sheet to make a bundle with a frilly top, pinching the dough closed above the soufflé. Set the wrapped soufflés aside on a baking sheet. Repeat the process 3 more times, each time setting the wrapped soufflés on the baking sheet. As soon as all the soufflés are wrapped, place the baking sheet in the oven and bake for 20 minutes. Otherwise, the wrapped soufflés may be returned to the freezer —they will keep for up to a week—and baked later. Transfer them straight from the freezer to the preheated oven; do not thaw them first.

While the soufflés are in the oven, prepare the fruit garnishes. In separate pans, heat the jams and strain those that contain seeds and thin those that are too thick with water to obtain the consistency of a sauce.

To serve, place dollops of the different sauces in a circle on a large plate, place the soufflé in the middle and serve immediately.

Chateau Souverain – Cafe at the Winery

Wine-country cooking takes on different meaning when you can savor it in a real, working winery. State law now restricts the opening of any new restaurant within a winery, but you can still enjoy this memorable experience at Chateau Souverain in Sonoma County's Alexander Valley.

As you mount the wide, winding steps up to the double-towered château, you will understand why both nineteenth-century and modern winery architects copied the elegance and grandeur of the European château wineries. Soon you'll be gazing out over the grapevines toward Mt. St. Helena or the Mayacamas Range and dining on modern translations of traditional wine-country fare created by Martin Courtman, the executive chef.

Born in Europe, Courtman was trained in London and gained experience in the demanding kitchens of the

Mansion on Turtle Creek in Dallas and the Carlyle Restaurant in Houston. He carefully matches his food to the wines of Chateau Souverain, which are available by the glass or bottle. A succulent roast Sonoma chicken is a staple of the menu, which usually includes such time-honored favorites as New York steak, roast leg of lamb, and grilled salmon fillet.

Courtman updates these well-known dishes with contemporary flavors, using local ingredients whenever possible. Roasted California walnuts, for example, may provide a smoky-flavored garnish for your salad of local organic greens and then contribute their dusky accents to the fresh rosemary butter melting on your steak. The dessert list is short but creative and provides an excellent excuse to linger over coffee while enjoying the extraordinary view.

LEEK AND POTATO SOUP WITH ANISE

Serves 8. Wine recommendation: a delicate floral Sauvignon Blanc with undertones of apple and pear

Chop the leek, using only a little of the green part, the onion, fennel and potatoes into uniformly small pieces so that they will cook evenly.

In a thick-bottomed pan, melt the butter and stir in the leeks, onion and fennel. Add the anise, thyme, parsley and bay leaves. Cover the pan with a lid and cook the vegetables, without allowing them to color, over a low heat for 5 minutes, stirring a couple of times. Add the potatoes and the stock and season lightly with salt and pepper. Raise the heat, bring the mixture to a boil and then simmer it for 30 minutes or until the potatoes are well cooked.

Strain the soup through a sieve and try to force all the ingredients through. You may purée the mixture in a blender first, but only for a few seconds—blending will change the texture of the potatoes—then strain the purée through the sieve.

Add the chopped dill to the sour cream and season with pinches of cayenne.

This soup may be served hot or cold. To serve it hot, pour the strained soup into a measuring container so that you can see how much soup base you have. For every quart of base, you will need 1/2 cup cream. (If you don't plan on serving all of the soup at once, hold off adding the cream until reheating.) Place the cream into a saucepan over moderate heat and reduce it by one-third. Then add the soup base to the cream, bring the mixture back to a boil, stirring occasionally, and season with salt and pepper to taste. If desired, the soup may be finished by whisking in 2 tablespoons soft butter for each quart of soup base. Pour the soup into 8 warmed soup bowls and garnish with the sour cream mixture and sprigs of fresh dill.

To serve the soup cold, chill the soup base thoroughly after straining it. For every quart of soup base, you will need 1/2 cup cream. Add the cream to the well-chilled soup base (there is no need to reduce the cream) and season with salt and pepper to taste. Chill 8 soup bowls, pour soup into each bowl and garnish with the sour cream mixture and sprigs of fresh dill.

1 medium leek, cleaned
1 yellow onion
1/2 pound bulbous fennel
1 1/2 pounds white potatoes, peeled
4 tablespoons unsalted butter
1 teaspoon anise seeds
1 small sprig of fresh thyme
6 stems of parsley
2 bay leaves
2 quarts chicken stock
Salt and freshly ground pepper
1 1/2 teaspoons chopped dill
1/4 cup sour cream
Pinch of cayenne pepper
4 to 8 tablespoons unsalted butter
   (optional)
1 to 2 cups cream
8 sprigs dill, for garnish

One 4 1/2-pound chicken
Salt and freshly ground black pepper
Half a lemon
6 sprigs rosemary, each 2 inches long
7 cups chicken stock
1 teaspoon potato flour
Approximately 2 tablespoons unsalted
   butter (optional)

Vegetable Couscous
1 1/2 tablespoons unsalted butter
1/4 cup finely chopped yellow onion
1/4 cup finely chopped leek, white part only
1/4 cup finely chopped celery
1/4 cup finely chopped carrot
3/4 cup chicken stock
1 bay leaf
Salt and freshly ground black pepper
3/4 cup couscous
1 tablespoon chopped parsley

ROASTED SONOMA CHICKEN WITH VEGETABLE COUSCOUS

Serves 4. Wine recommendation: a rich, buttery Chardonnay

Preheat the oven to 350 degrees F.

Remove the wishbone with a paring knife and any fat or parts left in the chicken cavity. Season the cavity with salt and pepper and place the half lemon and 2 of the sprigs of fresh rosemary inside. Truss the chicken so that heat will penetrate more evenly, juices will not be lost and the bird will look better.

Place the chicken on its back on a rack in a roasting pan. (The bird should not be placed directly onto the bottom of the pan.) Cook the chicken in the oven for 20 minutes, then lift it up with a long fork and pour off any juices onto the bottom of the pan. (These juices will caramelize, and you will use them later to make the gravy.) Place the chicken back into the oven, still on its back, and repeat this decanting process every 20 minutes until the chicken is done. If the chicken juices appear to be burning on the bottom of the pan rather than caramelizing, pour approximately 1/4 cup of chicken stock into the pan. You may do this only after the outside of the chicken is well sealed, at least 40 minutes into the cooking. The chicken should take approximately 1 hour and 20 minutes to cook (approximately 18 minutes per pound). A meat thermometer, inserted into the leg joint, should read 170 degrees F when the chicken is done. If you do not have a meat thermometer, check the juices at the end of the cooking time to be sure that they are clear.

Bring 6 cups of the chicken stock to a simmer in a small saucepan. Once the chicken is ready, take it out of the oven, remove it from the pan but leave it on the rack, and let it rest at room temperature for 20 minutes; this prevents the juices from running out as they would if carved prematurely. While the chicken is resting, make the gravy.

Carefully pour off any clear fat from the roasting pan, being sure to save the chicken juices. Place the roasting pan on a burner over low heat and caramelize the remaining juices; cook until almost all the moisture has evaporated. Turn up the heat and add 1 cup of chicken stock to dissolve the caramelized juices. Use a wooden spoon to loosen browned bits from the bottom of the pan. Continue stirring and adding stock in 1-cup increments when the previous cup has reduced by half until you have used up 6 cups.

Make a flour slurry by mixing the potato flour with the remaining 1 cup cold chicken stock in a glass. Add the flour slurry to the gravy pan and bring the mixture to a boil. Cook until the gravy is as thick as you like it. Season with salt and pepper and strain. You may enrich it, if desired, by adding 2 tablespoons butter for every cup of gravy.

Vegetable Couscous

In a small saucepan, melt the butter over medium heat. Add the onion, leek, celery and carrot. Cook for 2 minutes without browning the vegetables. Pour in the chicken stock, add the bay leaf and bring the mixture to a boil. Season with salt and pepper. Add the couscous, turn off the heat and stir the contents of the pan with a fork. Cover the saucepan and put it in a warm place for 15 minutes. Then add the chopped parsley and taste for seasoning, stirring the couscous with a fork to keep it fluffy. If you are not ready to serve the couscous, replace the lid and set the pan aside in a warm spot. *Serves 4.*

To serve, remove the trussing string from the chicken, and cut off both legs and the breast. Separate the drumsticks from the thigh joint. Cut each breast in 2 equal parts and place a piece of dark and light meat on each plate. Pour the gravy over each portion and garnish with a sprig of rosemary. Serve with vegetable couscous.

ALMOND SHORTCAKE WITH SEASONAL BERRIES

1/3 cup finely chopped almonds

1 1/2 cups flour, less 2 tablespoons

1/2 teaspoon salt

2 1/2 teaspoons baking powder

1/2 cup sugar

6 tablespoons cold unsalted butter, cut into small pieces

1/2 cup buttermilk (set aside 2 tablespoons for brushing the top before baking)

Berry Mixture

3 cups hulled strawberries, blackberries or raspberries

2 tablespoons sugar, or more, to taste

1/2 teaspoon freshly squeezed lemon juice

Whipped cream, sweetened with sugar

Sprigs of mint, for garnish

Serves 4. Wine recommendation: a full-flavored, slightly sweet Gewürztraminer with nuances of honey and spice

Preheat the oven to 350 degrees F, and if your baking sheet does not have a nonstick surface, line it with parchment paper.

Mix the almonds, flour, salt, baking powder and 6 tablespoons of the sugar in a mixing bowl, using the paddle attachment of your mixer. On a slow speed, add the butter and mix for 2 minutes. Continuing on low speed, add the buttermilk. Mix only until the dough comes together.

Remove the dough from the bowl, place it on a lightly floured board and roll it out 1 1/2 inches thick. The dough will be stiff. Cut out 4 circles, each 3 inches across. Place the circles on a baking sheet and brush the tops with the reserved 2 tablespoons of buttermilk. Sprinkle the remaining 2 tablespoons of sugar on top. Bake for 25 minutes; the shortcakes are done when they are a light brown.

Berry Mixture

While the shortcakes are baking, prepare the berries. Purée 1 cup of the berries and strain the purée to remove any seeds. Add the rest of the berries (if you are using strawberries, you may wish to halve or quarter them, depending on their size) and mix gently to coat the whole berries with the purée. Adjust flavor to taste by adding the sugar and the lemon juice a little at a time. Stir gently. Refrigerate until ready to use.

To serve, cut each shortcake in half horizontally. Place the bottom halves on the serving plates and spoon the berry mixture over them. Place the top half of the shortcake a little off center. Garnish with whipped cream and mint.

Mendocino County

The Boonville Hotel

The little town of Boonville, in the middle of Mendocino's Anderson Valley, has gained international attention for its local dialect, known as "Boont." (Check out the downtown "Bucky Walter," elsewhere known as a pay phone.) Boonville is also the home of The Boonville Hotel, which is fast gathering a fame of its own for the fresh, spontaneous cooking of Johnny Schmidt, served up in a friends-and-family atmosphere that embraces valley residents, first-time guests, and regular visitors.

"We never planned to be cutting edge or trendy, because people come to this area for a simpler approach to life," Schmidt points out. "We focus on simple preparations, hearty ingredients, and friendly service." The menu changes several times a week, partly due to necessity. "It's fairly last minute because I never know what I'm preparing until the ingredients arrive. Winter brings heartier fare, such as ragouts and soups. Summer brings more grilled fish, salsas, and simple fruit desserts."

A weekly farmers' market right outside the Hotel and his sister's apple farm just down the highway provide Schmidt with many of his raw materials. He then puts the menu together, drawing on his love for Mexico and his formal culinary training in France.

The feeling at the Boonville Hotel, though, is always downhome. Schmidt grew up in the Napa Valley, where his parents operated the famed French Laundry restaurant. To launch the Hotel, Schmidt had to complete major renovations on the existing structure. His staff then came over from Schmidt's former place, the tiny Floodgate Cafe in nearby Navarro, and local artisans provided the furniture and decor—including the pig mascot hanging by the kitchen door.

ROASTED VEGETABLE BISQUE WITH THYME

Serves 6. Wine recommendation: a dry Gewürztraminer

2 red bell peppers, seeded and coarsely
  chopped
2 white or yellow onions, coarsely chopped
2 to 3 cloves garlic, chopped
2 to 3 razor-thin lemon slices
3 tablespoons fresh thyme
1 bay leaf
Half a jalapeño pepper, chopped (optional)
Salt and freshly ground black pepper
2 tablespoons balsamic vinegar
4 tablespoons virgin olive oil
2 slices stale French bread, broken up
1 sprig fresh rosemary
3 cups canned tomatoes in juice (in season,
  you can use very ripe tomatoes)
3 cups chicken stock
1 cup dry white or red wine
1/4 cup sour cream, thinned with 2 or 3
  tablespoons half-and-half
Chopped parsley, for garnish

Preheat the oven to 400 degrees F.

Arrange the bell peppers, onions, garlic and lemon in a roasting pan. Season with half the thyme, half the bay leaf, the jalapeño, if using, and salt and pepper. Sprinkle the vinegar and 2 tablespoons of the oil over the vegetables. Roast the vegetables in the oven for 25 to 30 minutes until they start to brown.

Toast the French bread until it is brown and dry. Put the bread and the roasted vegetable mixture into a large soup pot with the remaining thyme and bay leaf, the rosemary, the remaining olive oil, the tomatoes, stock and wine. Cook over medium heat for 20 to 25 minutes until the mixture starts to thicken. Remove it from the heat. Purée the soup in a blender at high speed and strain through a sieve.

Season the soup with salt and pepper and garnish with a swirl of thinned sour cream and the parsley.

ROAST PORK LOIN IN RED CHILE AND OREGANO WITH SOFT POLENTA

2 cloves garlic, finely minced

2 dried *pasilla* or *ancho* chiles, coarsely ground

2 teaspoons fresh oregano, coarsely chopped

1 teaspoon sea salt (preferably flaked sea salt)

2 teaspoons coarsely ground fresh black pepper

3 pounds boneless, center-cut pork loin

Juice of 1 orange

Juice of 1 lime

Soft Polenta

6 cups unsalted chicken stock

1 small white onion, finely minced

1/4 cup minced red bell pepper

1 bay leaf

1 teaspoon salt

2 teaspoons finely minced jalapeño pepper

1 1/2 cups yellow polenta

4 tablespoons salted butter

Zest of 1 orange, chopped

1/4 cup finely minced green onions

Salt and freshly ground pepper

Wedges of lime, for garnish

Serves 6. Wine recommendation: a light, young Zinfandel or Pinot Noir

Preheat the oven to 425 degrees F.

Mix the garlic, chiles, oregano, salt and pepper together in a small bowl. Place the pork in a roasting pan and rub the spice mixture on the surface of the meat. Roast the pork in the oven for 10 to 20 minutes, depending on the size of the meat. Pour the citrus juices over the pork, reduce the oven temperature to 325 degrees F and continue to cook for 40 minutes to an hour.

While the pork is cooking, make the polenta.

Soft Polenta

In a large saucepan, bring to a rolling boil the chicken stock, onion, bell pepper, bay leaf, salt and jalapeño. Slowly add the polenta, whisking constantly. Reduce the heat to medium and continue to cook for 5 minutes or until the mixture has thickened. Stir in the butter, zest and green onions. Remove the pan from the heat, cover it and let sit for 10 minutes. This polenta will hold well for up to 1 hour if kept warm and tightly covered.

Pierce the meat with a sharp knife to see if the juices run clear. When the meat is cooked, remove it from the oven and let it rest for 15 minutes. Strain the pan juices, season them with salt and pepper and reserve. Slice the pork and serve it, with the meat juices, over soft polenta and garnish with wedges of lime.

CRANBERRY KUCHEN WITH HOT CREAM SAUCE

Serves 8. Wine recommendation: a crémant or slightly sweet sparkling wine

3/4 cup sugar

1/3 cup vegetable shortening

1 egg

3/4 cup half-and-half

1/4 teaspoon vanilla extract

1 3/4 cups flour

2 teaspoons baking powder

1/2 teaspoon salt

1/2 teaspoon freshly grated nutmeg

Zest of 1 orange, chopped

2 cups cranberries

1/2 cup chopped walnuts

Cinnamon and sugar

Hot Cream Sauce

2 cups heavy cream

1/2 cup sugar

4 tablespoons unsalted butter

Zest of 1 orange, chopped

Preheat the oven to 375 degrees F and grease a 9-inch pie pan.

Cream the sugar and the shortening in a mixer until smooth. Add the egg and beat for 2 to 3 minutes. Add the half-and-half and vanilla and beat until the mixture is smooth.

Sift the flour, baking powder, salt and nutmeg together and add the mixture to the wet ingredients, combining them on low speed. Add the zest. Gently fold in 1 cup of the cranberries.

Pour the batter into the pan and arrange the remaining cranberries in the center and the walnuts around the cranberries. Sprinkle with cinnamon and sugar and bake for 35 to 40 minutes until the *kuchen* is done in the center.

Hot Cream Sauce

While the *kuchen* is baking, prepare the hot cream sauce. Combine the cream, sugar, butter and zest in a heavy saucepan and cook over medium heat until the mixture is boiling. Reduce the liquid for approximately 10 minutes, watching carefully to prevent it from boiling over. Just before serving, heat the sauce and whisk it.

Slice the *kuchen* and serve with the hot cream sauce.

St. Orres

The onion-shaped dome of St. Orres flashes coppery red as the sun sets along the Pacific coast in the sleepy southern Mendocino town of Gualala. The Russian-style dome is just as dramatic inside, for it covers a three-story dining room with hanging vines and interior balconies. The drama continues with the sumptuous, wild, and whimsical cooking of Rosemary Campiformio, the chef and co-owner.

"I am blessed to be living in an area that still provides its residents the gift of wild food," says Campiformio, who is also St. Orres's certified mushroom forager. "My inspiration comes from the magic of the forest, the mystery of the ocean, and the wonder of the rivers." The bounty along the Pacific coast provides Campiformio with mushrooms and berries, wild boar and venison, salmon and scallops—the list is long and varied.

Campiformio brings to her wild ingredients a polished sophistication and a sense of culinary humor. She has been known to match "red hot" candies with jicama in a butter lettuce salad, and her signature tequila, Kahlua, and pine nut ice cream is not to be missed. After-dinner tea selections include pine needle, Douglas fir, and wild fennel.

The flavors that come out of the kitchen at St. Orres are rich and complementary, and the atmosphere and service add greatly to the enjoyment. Those in the know alternate full dinners in the dining room with more casual, à la carte dining in the candlelit, glassed-in patio off the bar where you can get most items from the main menu and possibly things that aren't even on the menu. St. Orres is also a cozy, other-worldly inn, with accommodations upstairs in the main building and in snug cottages scattered among the surrounding trees.

SEAFOOD WITH SAFFRON PASTA AND SEAWEED

Serves 4. Wine recommendation: a crisp Chardonnay or Sémillon

Saffron Pasta

Saffron Pasta

3 cups flour

4 eggs

1 1/2 teaspoons powdered saffron

Pinch of salt

3 tablespoons olive oil

2 tablespoons unsalted butter

1 tablespoon chopped garlic

16 scallops (8 shucked, 8 in the shell)

8 large shrimp, with heads and shells on

Salt and freshly ground white pepper,
    to taste

2 cups Chardonnay

1 cup finely diced fresh tomato

8 mussels, in the shell

4 whole fresh squid, cleaned and cut
    into rings

1/4 cup finely chopped fresh cilantro

3 sheets *nori,** shredded, for garnish

3 teaspoons *tobiko,** for garnish

*Nori is available in jars in Asian
markets and health food stores. *Tobiko*
is flying fish roe and can also be found
in Asian markets.

Mound the flour on a clean work surface and make a well in the center. In a bowl, using a fork, mix together the eggs and saffron. Pour this mixture into the well and gradually incorporate the flour. Form the dough into a ball and knead it with the palm of your hand. Knead for approximately 8 minutes. The dough should be smooth and elastic. Cover with a clean towel and set it aside to rest for 15 minutes. Divide the dough into fourths. Using a hand-cranked pasta machine, roll the dough out into thin sheets and cut each sheet with the fettuccine attachment.

To cook the pasta, bring a large pot of water to the boil. Add the pinch of salt and 1 tablespoon of the olive oil. Add the pasta and cook until it reaches the desired tenderness, approximately 5 minutes. Drain the cooked pasta, place it in a large pasta bowl with the remaining 2 tablespoons olive oil and toss.

While the pasta is cooking, melt the butter in a saucepan over low heat, add the garlic and sauté lightly. Season the shucked scallops and the shrimp with the salt and pepper. Increase the heat to high and sear the shrimp and the scallops for approximately 1 minute per side. The scallops will acquire a crust and the shrimp will turn pink. Remove the scallops and shrimp and keep them warm. To the garlic and butter in the saucepan, add the wine, tomato, mussels and the scallops in the shell. Cover the pan, bring the contents to a boil and allow the shellfish to steam open, approximately 3 minutes. The shellfish will be done when the shells are open and the meat is firm but still plump. Add the seared scallops, cooked shrimp and squid rings and continue cooking for 2 minutes. Remove all the seafood from the saucepan and arrange it in the center of the pasta. Return the pan with the liquid to a high flame and add the cilantro. Bring the mixture to a boil. Taste and season with salt and pepper. Pour it on the seafood, garnish with the *nori* and *tobiko* and serve immediately.

Stuffing

4 tablespoons unsalted butter
1 andouille sausage, diced
1 small red onion, finely diced
1 leek, white part only, finely diced
1 stalk celery, finely diced
1 cup wild mushrooms,* finely chopped
3 cups fresh bread crumbs
Pinch of dried thyme
Pinch of dried sage
1 teaspoon chopped parsley
1 1/2 cups chicken stock

8 quail, breast bones removed
Peanut oil
Salt and freshly ground black pepper

Yam Waffles

1 cup flour
1 teaspoon baking powder
1/2 teaspoon baking soda
1/2 cup cooked, mashed yam
  (1 medium yam)
1 cup buttermilk
2 eggs, separated
2 tablespoons unsalted butter, melted
  and cooled

8 whole wild mushrooms,* for garnish
1 tablespoon peanut oil
16 quail eggs, for garnish
1/4 cup real maple syrup

*Never eat or serve a wild mushroom
unless you obtain it from a reputable
source or, if you have picked it yourself,
until you have had it positively identified.

WILD MUSHROOM–STUFFED QUAIL WITH SWEET YAM WAFFLES

Serves 4. Wine recommendation: a fruity, spicy Merlot

Stuffing

Melt the butter in a large sauté pan. Sauté the sausage, onion, leek and celery over high heat until the onions and celery are cooked through, approximately 5 minutes. Add the wild mushrooms and continue cooking for 2 minutes. Remove the pan from the heat and add the bread crumbs, thyme, sage and parsley. Add 1 cup of the chicken stock to moisten the mixture and set aside to cool.

Preheat the oven to 350 degrees F.

Close the neck opening of the quail with toothpicks. Stuff the cavity of each quail with 3 tablespoons of the cooled stuffing. Secure the cavity opening with toothpicks.

Coat a large sauté pan with peanut oil and heat on high. Season the quail with salt and pepper and brown them on all sides. Transfer the quail to an ovenproof dish, add the remaining 1/2 cup chicken stock and bake in the oven until the quail are cooked through, approximately 20 minutes.

Yam Waffles

Preheat a lightly greased waffle iron.

In a large mixing bowl, combine the flour, baking powder and baking soda and set aside. Place the yam and buttermilk into a food processor, and process until the mixture is smooth. In a separate bowl, stir together the egg yolks and melted butter and add the yam mixture. In another bowl beat the egg whites until they are stiff. Stir the yam mixture into the dry ingredients quickly, mixing until smooth. Gently fold in the beaten egg white.

For each waffle, pour approximately 3/4 cup batter onto the waffle iron. (This amount may vary, depending on the size of your waffle iron.) Bake for approximately 5 minutes or until the steaming stops. Keep the cooked waffles warm in a low oven. *Makes 4 waffles.*

Prepare the garnishes by steaming the whole mushrooms until they wilt, set them aside and keep them warm. To fry the quail eggs, heat the peanut oil in a frying pan on high. Turn the heat off, crack the eggs carefully into the oil and fry them. The residual heat in the pan is enough to cook the eggs perfectly.

To serve, cut each waffle in half on the diagonal, place the 2 pieces on a plate and dribble the syrup on top. Place 2 quail on top of the waffles. Garnish the plates with wild mushrooms and the fried quail eggs, sunny-side up.

WILD HUCKLEBERRY TART

Serves 8 to 10. Wine recommendation: a Zinfandel Port

Tart Filling

4 cups wild huckleberries
1/4 cup sifted flour
3/4 cup sugar
1 tablespoon unsalted butter, cut into
    small pieces

Pastry

3 cups flour
2 teaspoons baking powder
1 cup (2 sticks) unsalted butter
1 cup sugar
2 eggs

Tart Filling

Preheat the oven to 350 degrees F.

Put the huckleberries into a large mixing bowl and sprinkle them with the flour, sugar and butter. Toss the huckleberries until they are completely covered. Set aside.

Pastry

In a medium-sized bowl, combine the flour and baking powder. Cream together the butter and sugar in the bowl of an electric mixer. Add the eggs. With the mixer at medium speed, gradually add the flour mixture. Mix for approximately 2 minutes or until the dough starts to hold together. Remove the dough from the mixing bowl and form it into a ball. Divide the dough in half. Using your hands, gently pat one half of the dough into a rectangular 7 1/2-by-11-by-1-inch tart pan, covering the bottom and sides evenly. Fill the pastry shell with the tart filling. With the remaining half of the pastry dough, make small crumbs and arrange them on top of the huckleberries to cover.

Bake the tart for approximately 45 minutes or until it is golden brown and the juices have thickened.

The Ledford House Restaurant

It takes a while to get over the view at the Ledford House Restaurant. From the dining room, you can watch the ocean crashing against the rocks below. There's no better place to order a dozen oysters, drink champagne and watch the sun set. Once it's dark at last, the action turns inward to the blond-wood bar, the white linen tablecloths, and the candlelight reflected in the windows.

Seduced by the wildness and romance of the Mendocino coast, the proprietors Lisa and Tony Geer bought the Ledford House Restaurant in 1987 after running a small cafe in the Feather River forests of northeastern California. "Neither of us have formal restaurant training," Tony admits. "We survived on our passion for cooking, with constant feedback from our eclectic clientele."

At the Ledford House Restaurant, the Geers revel in the wide range of fresh ingredients available on the coast near the wine-producing Anderson Valley. "The abundance of small farms, fresh fish, berries, and wild mushrooms puts us in a culinary whirlwind that we still fly in today," Tony says. For evidence, he garnishes a salad of baby greens with freshly picked wildflowers, a melon soup with plum purée, and a grilled salmon with fried sage.

"We think of our food in terms of color, texture, and flavor and try to share our excitement with our customers," say the Geers. That sharing begins as customers arrive and receive a warm greeting. "For some," Tony says with a smile, "eating is an art in itself."

GRAVLAX OF HALIBUT WITH CITRUS VINAIGRETTE

Serves 6. Wine recommendation: a dry Gewürztraminer

1/2 cup sugar
1/2 cup kosher or coarse salt
1/2 teaspoon ground ginger
1/2 teaspoon ground black pepper
1 pound fresh halibut fillet
1 bunch fresh baby dill, chopped fine

Citrus Vinaigrette
2 tablespoons lemon juice
2 tablespoons orange juice
1/2 tablespoon balsamic vinegar
1/4 teaspoon salt
3/4 cup olive oil

A Note on Procedure
You will need to start the gravlax a day before you plan to serve it.

Blend the sugar, salt, ginger and pepper in a bowl and coat the fillet with the mixture. Sprinkle the dill over both sides of the fish and place the fish and the sugar mixture in a plastic bag. Refrigerate the fish for at least 24 hours. The halibut should look translucent when done. Wipe the excess dill and sugar mixture off the fillet. Using an extremely sharp fillet or chef's knife, slice the fish at a 45-degree angle to get wafer-thin slices.

Citrus Vinaigrette
Place the lemon and orange juices, vinegar, salt and oil in a blender and mix them well. *Makes 1/2 cup.*

To serve, spoon some citrus vinaigrette on a plate and arrange 3 or 4 rolled up thin slices of the halibut on top.

GRILLED SALMON WITH AVOCADO BUTTER AND FRIED SAGE

1/4 cup olive oil

12 large fresh sage leaves

2 medium avocados

1/2 cup (1 stick) unsalted butter, softened

Juice of 1 lime

Salt and freshly ground black pepper

6 salmon fillets (6 ounces each), skin on

Serves 6. Wine recommendation: a fruity Pinot Noir

Prepare a hot grill.

In a small sauté pan, heat the olive oil over medium heat, fry the sage leaves quickly and transfer them to paper towels. (Be careful to stand back—the hot oil may splatter.) Reserve the oil for basting the salmon.

Peel and pit the avocados. Place them in a food processor with the butter and lime juice; process until the mixture is smooth. Season to taste with salt and pepper.

Baste the salmon with the reserved oil, season with salt and pepper and grill the fillets, skin side down, for 4 minutes. Turn the fish and cook for 3 minutes on the other side. When the fish is cooked, peel off the skin.

To serve, transfer the fish to 6 warm plates, top with avocado butter and garnish with the fried sage leaves.

CHOCOLATE TRUFFLE TORTE WITH RASPBERRY PURÉE AND CHANTILLY CREAM

1 pound plus 6 ounces bittersweet chocolate

1/4 cup dark rum

1 double espresso or 1 1/2 teaspoons
    instant espresso

2/3 cup walnuts

1/4 cup confectioners' sugar

1 1/4 cups cake flour

1/4 teaspoon salt

1 cup plus 2 tablespoons (2 1/4 sticks)
    unsalted butter, softened

3/4 cup granulated sugar

5 large eggs, separated

2 teaspoons vanilla extract

6 tablespoons unsalted butter

Raspberry Purée

2 baskets fresh raspberries

1/4 cup confectioners' sugar, sifted,
    or as needed

Chantilly Cream

1 cup heavy cream

1/4 cup confectioners' sugar, sifted

1 teaspoon vanilla extract

Serves 10. Wine recommendation: a big, chewy, fruity Cabernet Sauvignon or framboise liqueur

Position a rack in the center of the oven and preheat the oven to 350 degrees F. Butter a 10-inch round cake pan and dust it with flour.

In the top of a double boiler over hot, but not boiling, water, melt the 1 pound of chocolate with the rum and espresso, stirring frequently until the mixture is smooth. Remove the mixture from the heat and allow it to cool until it is tepid.

Process the walnuts and confectioners' sugar in a food processor for 10 to 20 seconds or until the walnuts are coarsely ground. Add the flour and salt and pulse 4 or 5 times until the ingredients are blended. Transfer the mixture to a medium bowl.

In a separate bowl, beat the butter and the granulated sugar with an electric mixer for 3 to 5 minutes or until creamy. Add the egg yolks and vanilla and beat for 50 to 60 seconds longer, or until the mixture is light in color. Blend in the melted chocolate mixture.

In another bowl, beat the egg whites until they begin to form soft peaks. Fold one third of the egg whites along with one-third of the walnut mixture into the chocolate mixture. Fold in the remainder of the walnut mixture and the egg whites in 2 more increments. Transfer the batter to the prepared pan and bake the torte for approximately 35 minutes. The torte should be moist in the center and just beginning to shrink from the sides of the pan. Do not overbake. Let the torte cool in its pan on a wire rack for 20 to 30 minutes, then remove it from the pan and set it to finish cooling on the wire rack.

While the torte is cooling, make the chocolate glaze. Melt the remaining 6 ounces of chocolate in a double boiler, then whisk in the 6 tablespoons of butter, 1 tablespoon at a time. Place the torte, still on the rack, on a baking sheet to catch the glaze as it drips. Pour the glaze over the cooled torte and allow the chocolate to set. When set (the process may be accelerated by placing the cake in the refrigerator for a few minutes), transfer the cake to a serving platter.

Raspberry Purée

Purée the raspberries in a food processor and run the purée through a fine sieve to remove the seeds. Sweeten to taste with confectioners' sugar.

Chantilly Cream

Combine the cream, sugar and vanilla in a bowl and whip until soft peaks form.

To serve, spoon raspberry purée onto a plate, place a slice of torte in the sauce and top with chantilly cream.

Albion River Inn

Steve Smith's first visit to the kitchen at his uncle's Albion River Inn was hardly an epiphany. "I had no great dreams of becoming a chef," he recalls. "I was just a kid interested in earning some money." Three years later, he had acquired the fundamentals of classic cooking and a vision of his future. After graduating from the California Culinary Academy and apprenticing at Stars in San Francisco, Smith returned to the Albion River Inn as head chef.

"I describe my cuisine as California, regional, and coastal," he says, "because I take full advantage of the harvest of the rural countryside and coastline: local wild mushrooms, fresh fruit and herbs, local seafood, and the best and most flavorful meats available." Smith's restaurant takes full advantage of its setting, perched above the mouth of the Albion River on the rugged Mendocino coast. A wrecked ship provided the rough timbers that give the Inn its seafaring charm.

The nearby Anderson Valley is fast becoming a producer of premium wines, and Smith is alert to the possibilities. "Living here certainly informs my cooking," he explains. "I use a Mistelle of an Anderson Valley Petite Sirah in my recipe for smoked pork loin. It's a perfect pairing of flavors."

Smith's robust flavors and the Inn's location make another good pair. "Along rural coastal roads, there is a sense of adventure in traveling through the night and then seeing the glow of the Inn's lights," Smith says. Those who end their adventure at the Albion River Inn will find hearty food in a cozy haven, often warmed by a crackling fire.

SESAME-SEARED SEA SCALLOPS WITH RISOTTO AND ORANGE-RIESLING SAUCE

Serves 4 to 6. Wine recommendation: a rich, off-dry Riesling or Gewürztraminer

Risotto

In a medium pot, add the water, salt and pepper, bring it to a boil and keep it hot.

In a heavy saucepan over medium heat, melt 2 tablespoons of the butter and sauté the onion, rice and ginger until the mixture is golden brown. Add 1 cup of the hot, seasoned water slowly, stirring the rice mixture.

When the first cup of water has been almost completely absorbed, stir in a second cup. Continue cooking the rice, adding the remaining water in increments until all the water has been absorbed; this will take approximately 20 minutes. Remove the pan from the heat, stir in the remaining 4 tablespoons butter, the lemon juice, cilantro and Parmesan cheese. Check the seasoning and correct if necessary. Keep the risotto warm.

Orange-Riesling Cream Sauce

Place the orange juice, Riesling, cream and ginger in a heavy pan. Stir and cook over medium-high heat until the sauce thickens and coats the back of a spoon. Remove the pan from the heat and stir in the cilantro. Season with salt and pepper. *Makes 1 cup.*

When you are ready to serve, reheat the sauce gently and prepare the scallops.

Remove the tough muscle from the scallops, season them with salt and pepper. Combine the flour and sesame seeds and roll the scallops in the mixture. Heat the oil in a shallow sauté pan over medium-high heat until it is very hot but not smoking. Cook the scallops until they are golden brown on both sides, turning them only once; this will take approximately 2 minutes per side.

To serve, spoon some of the heated sauce into the center of a warm wide-rimmed dinner plate, mound hot risotto in the center of the sauce and circle the rice with the hot scallops. Garnish with cilantro.

Risotto

4 cups water

1 teaspoon salt

1/2 teaspoon finely ground black pepper

6 tablespoons unsalted butter

1 yellow onion, minced

1 cup arborio rice

2 tablespoons peeled and minced fresh ginger

Juice of 1 lemon

1 tablespoon finely chopped fresh cilantro

1/2 cup grated Parmesan cheese

Orange-Riesling Cream Sauce

1 cup freshly squeezed orange juice

1/4 cup Riesling wine

1 cup heavy cream

1 tablespoon peeled and minced fresh ginger

1 tablespoon chopped fresh cilantro

Salt and freshly ground black pepper

1 pound fresh sea scallops

Salt and freshly ground black pepper

1/3 cup flour

1/3 cup sesame seeds

Peanut oil, for frying

Fresh cilantro, for garnish

3 tablespoons peeled and minced
  fresh ginger
3 tablespoons minced fresh garlic
  (1 small head)
1/2 cup soy sauce
1/2 cup red wine vinegar
1/2 cup honey
2 tablespoons salt
2 pounds pork loin or tenderloin

Wild Rice and Pasta Medley
1/4 cup olive oil
1/3 cup wild rice
1/3 cup long-grain white rice
1/3 cup orzo pasta
2 1/4 cups water
1 teaspoon salt
1/2 teaspoon freshly ground black pepper
1 tablespoon garlic powder

Huckleberry Sauce
1/2 cup fresh huckleberries, washed
  and drained
2 tablespoons minced shallots
1/2 cup *Mistelle* of Petite Sirah, crème
  de cassis, or a late-harvest red wine
1/2 cup beef stock
1/4 cup honey

16 whole *shiitake* mushroom caps
6 sprigs fresh cilantro

HOUSE-SMOKED PORK LOIN WITH HUCKLEBERRY SAUCE AND WILD RICE AND PASTA MEDLEY

Serves 4. Wine recommendation: a medium-bodied, well-balanced Pinot Noir

A Note on Procedure
The huckleberry sauce may be prepared a day ahead or while the pasta and rice medley is cooling. The meat may be brined and smoked a week ahead and refrigerated. If you don't have access to a smoker, purchase smoked pork loin at a specialty meat market.

In a deep nonreactive bowl, combine the ginger, garlic, soy sauce, vinegar, honey and salt. Add the pork, turning the meat to coat it and marinate overnight, turning once. Drain the pork and discard the brine.

Cold-smoke the pork over applewood for 2 hours, following the manufacturer's instructions for the smoker.

Wild Rice and Pasta Medley
In a heavy pot, heat the olive oil and sauté the rices and pasta until the grains are golden brown. Season the water with salt, pepper and garlic powder and add it to the rice. Bring the mixture to a boil, reduce the heat and keep it at a slow simmer. Cook, covered, for 25 minutes. Remove the pan from the heat and let it stand, covered, for 10 minutes.

Huckleberry Sauce
Place the berries, shallots, wine, stock and honey in a small heavy saucepan, stir and bring the mixture to a simmer over medium-high heat. Cook, stirring, until the liquid is reduced by half or until it coats a spoon; this will take approximately 8 to 10 minutes.

Slice the smoked pork thinly into 20 medallions. Grill the meat and mushrooms for 2 minutes on each side.

To serve, spoon hot huckleberry sauce onto warm plates, place the wild rice and pasta medley in the center and arrange the pork slices and mushroom caps alternately around the rice and pasta. Garnish with the cilantro.

APPLE-CRUMB COBBLER WITH VANILLA-BEAN ICE CREAM

Serves 4 to 6. Wine recommendation: Calvados or a superior apple brandy

Cobbler Filling

Preheat the oven to 350 degrees F.

In a large bowl, combine the apples, vanilla and lemon extracts, lemon juice, sugars, flour and butter and mix the ingredients thoroughly. Place the filling in an ungreased 8-by-8-by-2-inch baking dish.

Crumb Topping

In a medium-sized bowl, mix the flour, sugars, cinnamon and butter and rub the mixture between your fingers until it is crumbly. Spread the mixture over the filling and bake the cobbler for 45 to 50 minutes until it is golden brown on top and the apples are tender.

Vanilla-Bean Ice Cream

In a large heavy saucepan, combine the cream, milk, sugar and vanilla bean and stir until just brought to a simmer. Remove from the heat immediately.

Remove the vanilla bean and slice it in half lengthwise. Scrape out the seeds and return the seeds and any pulp to the scalded cream mixture; discard the bean pod.

Whisk together the egg yolks and lemon juice and temper them by adding a couple of tablespoons of the hot custard. Whisk the egg mixture into the custard and strain through a fine sieve. Following the manufacturer's directions, freeze the mixture in an ice-cream maker. *Makes 2 quarts.*

Serve the cobbler warm with a scoop of vanilla-bean ice cream.

Cobbler Filling

4 Granny Smith apples, peeled, cored
    and sliced
1 tablespoon vanilla extract
1 tablespoon lemon extract
Juice of 1 lemon
1/2 cup light brown sugar
1/2 cup granulated sugar
1/2 cup flour
8 tablespoons (1 stick) unsalted butter,
    cut into 16 pieces

Crumb Topping

1 cup flour
1/4 cup light brown sugar
1/4 cup granulated sugar
1 tablespoon ground cinnamon
8 tablespoons (1 stick) unsalted butter,
    cut into 32 pieces

Vanilla-Bean Ice Cream

2 cups heavy cream
2 cups whole milk
1 cup sugar
1 vanilla bean
4 egg yolks
Juice of 1 small lemon

Cafe Beaujolais

Toward the northwestern boundary of California's wine country, set above a rocky Pacific cove, is the wind-swept town of Mendocino. Home to a thriving artists' community, Mendo, as locals call it, resembles a New England fishing village. A stroll through its narrow streets, alive with the scents and sounds of the nearby ocean, is an ideal way to whet your appetite for a meal at Cafe Beaujolais. The inside of the Cafe is a lot like the town: a bustle of generous, graceful hospitality.

Margaret Fox, who owns the Cafe, arrived in Mendocino almost twenty years ago to work as a baker at the Mendocino Hotel. Soon after, she and friends purchased the Cafe and set out to create a style as distinctive as the town itself. "We started with an eclectic American breakfast, lunch, and dinner menu," Fox recalls, "the dinners being seasonal and cooked by myself." These days, Fox presides over the breakfasts and brunches that she calls "morning food"—the same ingredients other people eat for breakfast, she says, "put together in a different way."

Dinner is the province of Fox's husband, Christopher Kump, who came to Cafe Beaujolais in 1984 with a strong background in French cooking. On any given evening, though, Kump's menu may also be influenced by the cuisines of Italy, Japan, or Mexico.

No matter what's on the menu, the ingredients most likely came from a nearby, ecologically responsible farm or ranch. And as you enter, be sure to notice the edible blossoms and herbs growing outside the restaurant; their savory flavors may well be blended into your meal in unexpected ways.

MAPLE-GLAZED CHESTNUT AND WILD MUSHROOM RAGOUT

Serves 4. Wine recommendation: a crisp Chardonnay

You will need two small heavy-bottomed pans: one that will just hold all the chestnuts snugly in one layer and one that will hold the carrots and onions just as snugly. In the first, combine the chestnuts with 2/3 cup of the stock, 1 tablespoon of the butter, the maple syrup and a light seasoning of salt and pepper. In the second, put the onions, 1 tablespoon of the butter, another 2/3 cup of stock and another light seasoning of salt and pepper.

Simmer the chestnuts partially covered for 15 to 20 minutes. Remove the lid and cook for approximately 5 more minutes until the liquid is syrupy and the chestnuts are tender but not falling apart. Meanwhile, bring the contents of the onion pan to a boil, lower the heat to a simmer and cook the onions, covered, over low heat for 3 minutes. Add the carrots to the pan, increase the heat to medium and cook for another 3 minutes, partially covered. Increase the heat to high and cook for another 1 to 2 minutes, uncovered, shaking and swirling the pan until the liquid has reduced to a syrupy, shiny glaze coating the vegetables. Remove the pan from the heat and test one carrot and one onion to make sure they are tender (but not too soft). If they are not quite tender, return the pan to the heat, add a tablespoon or two of water and cook for another minute or two, partially covered, until they are done. Combine the onions and carrots with the chestnuts and set aside.

With a clean vegetable or pastry brush and dishtowel, brush and wipe the mushrooms clean. Be especially careful to brush away dirt in the gills (the undersurface of the caps). Any embedded grit can be cut away with a paring knife. If the mushrooms are large, cut them into large bite-sized pieces (halving, quartering or thickly slicing them lengthwise usually makes wild mushrooms most attractive and reminiscent of their original shape); if small, leave them whole.

Heat the remaining 4 teaspoons of butter in a sauté pan large enough to hold all the mushrooms (they can be slightly crowded at first, because they will shrink as they cook). If necessary, cook the mushrooms in two batches. When the foam subsides, add the mushrooms and sauté them quickly over high heat, stirring or tossing them frequently, for approximately 2 minutes until they are just beginning to soften. Season generously with salt and pepper and continue to sauté until they are tender. If the mushrooms have released much liquid, continue to cook them to reduce and concentrate their juices. Add the glazed vegetables and chestnuts and the parsley. Stir to mix and cook everything together for 1 to 2 more minutes to blend the flavors and heat the mixture through. If the ragout seems dry, add a little more stock or water. Taste for seasoning and adjust if necessary.

To serve, divide among warm plates and garnish with the chervil sprigs.

A Note on Peeling Chestnuts

Using a sharp paring knife, cut an X through the tough outer shell on the flat side of the chestnut and score the brown outer skin. Heat two cups of either canola oil or water in a small pan. If you are using oil, heat it to 320 degrees F and fry the chestnuts in batches of 4 to 5 for 3 minutes, or until their shells curl away the from the nut meat. If you are using water, bring it to the boil and blanch the chestnuts, also in small batches, for approximately a minute to loosen the shells and skin. With either method, peel away the outer shells and inner skins with a paring knife as soon as the chestnuts are cool enough to handle. They become harder to peel as they cool.

1 cup peeled chestnuts (10 to 12 ounces before peeling) *see note*

1 1/3 to 1 2/3 cups chicken or turkey stock

3 tablespoons plus 1 teaspoon unsalted butter

4 teaspoons maple syrup

Fine sea salt and freshly ground black pepper, to taste

12 pearl onions, peeled

8 baby carrots, peeled, with greens intact and trimmed to within 1/4 inch of the carrot

8 ounces (4 cups) mixed fresh wild mushrooms,* the drier the better

2 to 3 teaspoons freshly chopped flat-leaf Italian parsley or minced chives

1 small bunch fresh chervil, washed and broken into small sprigs

*The more varieties of mushrooms, the more interesting the textures and flavors of your ragout. If you are not, however, an experienced mushroom hunter, *never* eat or serve a wild mushroom unless you obtain it from a reputable source or, if you have picked it yourself, until you have had it positively identified. Remember, even experienced mushroom foragers abide by the adage "When in doubt, throw it out."

PAN-ROASTED HALIBUT WITH SOUPY WHITE BEANS AND WILTED KALE

Serves 4. Wine recommendation: a peppery Pinot Noir

A Note on Procedure

Start the beans 3 hours ahead.

Soupy White Beans

Soupy White Beans
1 pound (2 1/2 cups) navy beans
1 onion, peeled and chopped
6 cloves garlic, peeled and chopped
7 cups water
1 bay leaf
2 sprigs fresh thyme or 1 teaspoon dried
2 sprigs fresh oregano or 1 tablespoon dried Mexican oregano, ground
2 sprigs fresh *epazote** or 1 tablespoon dried and ground
2 1/4 teaspoons fine sea salt

1 1/2 pounds fresh halibut fillet, cut into 4 equal portions, each 1 inch thick
Fine sea salt and freshly ground black pepper, to taste
1 small bunch Italian parsley, leaves stripped and chopped, stems saved
1 bunch fresh thyme, leaves stripped and minced (1 tablespoon), stems saved
3 ounces prosciutto, cut into 1/4-inch dice
4 tablespoons unsalted butter
2 shallots, peeled and chopped
4 to 5 cloves garlic, peeled and minced
1 cup white wine
1 cup fish stock or clam juice
1 cup chicken stock
2 ripe tomatoes, peeled, seeded and cut into 1/2-inch dice (substitute canned if good fresh tomatoes are unavailable)
2 teaspoons anise liqueur, such as Pernod

Wilted Kale

4 quarts loosely packed kale, washed and stemmed
1/2 cup water
2 tablespoons peeled, grated fresh ginger
1/2 teaspoon fine sea salt

*Epazote is available sometimes fresh and usually dried in Mexican markets.

Soupy White Beans

Pick over the beans carefully to remove any bits of dirt or small stones; then rinse and drain them. Combine everything except the salt in the top of a double boiler or in a heavy-bottomed pot over very low heat. Cook the mixture slowly, covered, for 2 1/2 to 3 hours until the bean skins are tender and the beans are soft. The mixture should stay soupy; add more water if it begins to get dry. When beans are fully cooked, the liquid should no longer be watery, but cloudy and thickened. Add the salt and continue to cook for another 15 minutes or so. Remove the herb sprigs before serving the beans.

If the beans are not to be served that day, stir them in order to cool them down as quickly as possible, then refrigerate the mixture. *Makes approximately 6 cups.*

Season the halibut fillets with salt and pepper. In a small bowl, mix the chopped parsley with half of the minced thyme (set aside 4 pinches of each for final garnishing), then sprinkle the herb mixture over the fish.

In a 2-quart saucepan over medium heat, sauté the prosciutto in 1 tablespoon of the butter for 3 to 5 minutes to render any fat and color it lightly. Add the shallots and cook for 2 to 3 minutes, or until softened. Add the garlic and the remaining minced thyme (except that reserved for garnish) and cook for another minute until the mixture is fragrant. Add the wine and herb stems and continue cooking until the liquid is reduced and glazes the shallots and prosciutto. Add the fish and chicken stocks and reduce the liquid to 1 cup. Remove the herb stems. Remove the pan from the heat and season the mixture with pepper (it should be sufficiently salted from the ham).

In a 10- or 12-inch skillet with a tight-fitting lid, combine the reduced cooking stock, the diced tomatoes, the anise liqueur and the remaining 3 tablespoons butter. Bring to a boil over high heat.

Wilted Kale

Cut the kale greens crosswise into 1 1/2-inch-wide ribbons. (If the leaves are especially large, cut them lengthwise first.) Combine the water, ginger and salt in a 12-inch skillet over medium-high heat. As soon as the water boils, add the kale, packing it down with the pan's lid. Cook, covered, over high heat until the kale is tender, approximately 5 to 7 minutes. Stir the greens and shake the pan several times while cooking to mix them. If the greens stick to the pan, add water, 1 tablespoon at a time. Cover and keep warm.

Add the fish fillets to the pan, cover it and cook over high heat for 2 to 3 minutes until the fish is cooked almost through—it should remain slightly soft to the touch and translucent at the center.

To serve, place the fillets on a bed of wilted kale and surround with warm, soupy white beans. Taste the pan sauce for seasoning, adjust if necessary and pour it over the halibut, trying to keep some of the tomatoes on top of the fish. Sprinkle with the reserved parsley and thyme mixture and serve.

1 1/4 pounds tart cooking apples, peeled,
    cored and cut into 8 to 12 pieces,
    depending on size (approximately
    3 to 4 apples, equaling 1 pound
    net weight after trimming)
1 tablespoon lemon juice
3 tablespoons Calvados or good-quality
    domestic apple brandy
1 cup plus 2 tablespoons sugar
2 large eggs, lightly beaten
6 tablespoons cake or pastry flour
3/4 cup heavy cream
1 teaspoon vanilla extract
1/2 cup unsalted butter, melted but not hot
Whipped cream, for serving

CARAMELIZED APPLE CLAFOUTIS WITH CALVADOS

Serves 4 to 6. Wine recommendation: a late-harvest Gewürztraminer

Preheat the oven to 400 degrees F and butter a 9-inch pie pan or an 8-by-8-inch coffee-cake pan.

In a medium bowl, toss the apple pieces with the lemon juice and 2 tablespoons of the Calvados.

Measure out 2/3 cup of the sugar and set it aside for caramelizing the apples. Beat the eggs with the remaining sugar for 1 to 2 minutes in a mixer until the mixture whitens and doubles in volume. Stir in the flour, cream, vanilla and the remaining tablespoon of Calvados; whisk until smooth. Pour 1 1/2 cups of the batter into the pan and bake for 5 to 6 minutes on the lower rack until it is just beginning to set but is not yet browned.

Meanwhile, caramelize the apples. Put 1/4 cup of the butter in a 10- to 12-inch skillet along with the reserved 2/3 cup of sugar. Cook over high heat, stirring to prevent the sugar from burning, until it caramelizes, approximately 2 minutes. Lift the apple pieces from the bowl, reserving the lemon juice and Calvados, and add the pieces to the skillet all at once. Swirl the pan to stop the sugar from coloring. Cook the apples over high heat, swirling the pan and stirring as necessary to prevent sticking. Continue until the apple pieces are puffed and clinging to one another and the juices are richly colored, approximately 8 to 10 minutes.

Remove the skillet from the heat, add the reserved lemon juice and Calvados mixture and cover briefly to trap the vapors. Transfer the apples to the baking pan and spread them out evenly on top of the half-cooked batter.

Raise the oven temperature to 475 degrees F. Whisk the remaining 1/4 cup melted butter gradually into the remaining batter and pour this mixture over the apples. Return the pan to the oven and bake for another 12 to 15 minutes until the top is set and lightly browned all over.

Remove the *clafoutis* from the oven and allow it to cool for 15 to 20 minutes. Serve warm with whipped cream.

955 Ukiah Street Restaurant

Peggy and Jamie Griffith recall the night they had just one guest for dinner at their Little River Restaurant, due to a storm on the Mendocino coast. "What else could we do," Peggy says, "but sit down, open some good wine, and all have dinner together?" Chances are you won't be alone when you visit the Griffiths' new restaurant at 955 Ukiah Street in the town of Mendocino, but you will get the same warm welcome.

"People come to Mendocino from all over to recharge their batteries," Peggy explains. "Couples renew themselves, smell the roses. Whether they are dining frugally or like kings, we want our guests to be welcome, comfortable, and relaxed." You'll begin to unwind just walking down 955 Ukiah's garden-lined brick path nestled between tall water towers. The former artist's studio was also a coffeehouse

and a community center before it became a restaurant, and the Griffiths have retained the exposed beams, high ceilings, and huge windows.

A similar openness favors the food, with dishes such as steamed mussels bathed in garlic and wine and ravioli filled with red chard and spinach. "We try to present fresh ingredients so that individual flavors stand up and become enhanced, rather than get overwhelmed or muddy," Jamie says. And with a reasonably priced wine list, selected from the local wineries, Jamie tries to encourage his guests to complement their meal with a glass of wine. "Dishes with subtle flavors that hint of their existence, but won't declare their identities, might best be enjoyed with a glass of well-rounded Chardonnay. Other tastes are rough and wild, ready to go down with a big Cabernet."

ROASTED WHITE CORN AND RED BEET SOUP

Serves 6 to 8. Wine recommendation: a dry, grassy Sauvignon Blanc

1 yellow onion, peeled and quartered

1 large leek, white part only, quartered lengthwise, sliced 1/2 inch thick, washed and drained

2 red beets, peeled and quartered

1 quart water or chicken or vegetable stock

2 tablespoons thyme leaves

6 medium garlic cloves, peeled and chopped

2 ears white corn, husked

1 1/2 quarts half-and-half

Salt and freshly ground white pepper, to taste

1 cup plain lowfat yogurt (optional)

In a food processor, finely chop the onion, leek and beets in batches. Place the vegetables in a medium-sized saucepan, add the water and thyme, then bring the mixture to a boil and simmer it for 45 minutes. Add the garlic and simmer for 15 minutes more.

While the beet mixture is cooking, place the corn on the burner of a gas stove (if you have an electric stove, preheat a burner to medium high) and roast until kernels just begin to blacken. Rotate the corn with tongs until the ears are evenly roasted. Remove from heat and allow them to cool for approximately 5 minutes. Standing the corn cobs on end, slice the kernels from the cob. Break them apart with your fingers and set them aside in a bowl.

When the beet mixture is done, purée it with the cooking water in batches in a food processor until smooth, approximately 5 minutes. In a large double boiler, heat the half-and-half, then add the beet mixture and the corn. Season with salt and pepper.

Cook the soup very gently for 30 minutes to let the flavors blend. Adjust the seasoning. Whip the yogurt, if using, by hand with a fork.

To serve, pour the soup into heated bowls and garnish by floating yogurt squiggles on the top.

POACHED SALMON WITH TOMATO AND TARRAGON SAUCE

Serves 6 to 8. Wine recommendation: a dry, buttery Chardonnay

Fish Stock

2 quarts water

2 salmon heads (or other type of fish heads)

1 yellow onion

5 tablespoons salt

3 bay leaves

1 tablespoon fresh thyme or 1 teaspoon
  dried

1 tablespoon fresh dill or 1 teaspoon dried

2 tablespoons fresh parsley

1 teaspoon fennel seed

Tomato and Tarragon Sauce

1 cup Chardonnay, or other white
  wine

3 shallots, peeled and finely chopped

1 tablespoon unsalted butter

12 sprigs fresh tarragon, leaves chopped
  coarsely, or 2 teaspoons dried

2 tomatoes,* puréed

Salt and freshly ground white pepper,
  to taste

4 pounds fresh salmon fillet, boned and
  skinned

*Fresh, organic, vine-ripened tomatoes
are essential. If they are not available, use
10 rehydrated sun-dried tomato halves.

Fish Stock

Place the water, salmon heads, onion and salt into a medium-sized pot, bring the contents to a boil, then turn down the heat and simmer the mixture for 30 minutes. Add the bay leaves, thyme, dill, parsley and fennel seeds and simmer for another 30 minutes.

Strain the stock into a deep skillet and set it aside.

Tomato and Tarragon Sauce

Combine the wine and shallots in a small saucepan, bring the liquid to a boil and reduce it to approximately 3 tablespoons. Remove the pan from heat and whisk in the butter and half the tarragon. Add the tomato and season with salt and pepper.

Slice the salmon at a 30-degree angle across the grain into 1/4-inch-thick medallions. Heat the stock until it is simmering and poach the fish in batches, 1 layer deep, until it is barely cooked; not more than 2 minutes.

To serve, place portions of salmon in the center of warm plates, spoon the tomato and tarragon sauce around the fish and sprinkle the remaining tarragon over the top.

MANGO MOUSSE WITH HUCKLEBERRY SAUCE

Serves 6 to 8. Wine recommendation: a semi-sweet Gewürztraminer with grapefruit flavors or sparkling wine

Peel the mangoes, chop them coarsely and purée them in a food processor. You should have about 3 cups of purée. Add the yogurt and 1/3 cup of the sugar. Blend until smooth. In a large bowl, whip the cream until it is stiff. Fold the mango mixture into the cream, then refrigerate the mousse until it is cold.

In a saucepan, stir together the huckleberries, the remaining 2/3 cup of sugar and the cornstarch, then add the water. Bring the mixture to a boil and simmer it for 20 to 30 minutes until the berries are soft. Strain the mixture, discard the solids and refrigerate the sauce.

To serve, place 1 tablespoon of huckleberry sauce into the bottom of a sundae or wine glass, fill to the halfway mark with mango mousse, cover that with 3 tablespoons of sauce, add another layer of mango mousse and top with 1 spoonful of sauce. Top with fresh berries, if desired.

3 ripe mangoes

1 cup plain low-fat yogurt

1 cup sugar

3/4 cup heavy cream

4 1/2 cups huckleberries, blueberries, blackberries or other berries

1 1/2 teaspoons cornstarch

1 cup water

Fresh berries, for garnish (optional)

DIRECTORY OF RESTAURANTS

Albion River Inn
3790 North Highway 1
Albion, California 95410
707-937-1919

All Seasons Cafe and Wine Shop
1400 Lincoln Avenue
Calistoga, California 94515
707-942-9111

Auberge du Soleil
180 Rutherford Hill Road
Napa, California 94573
707-963-1211

Bistro Don Giovanni
4110 St. Helena Highway (Hwy. 29)
Napa, California 94558
707-224-3300 or 800-348-5406

Bistro Ralph
109 Plaza Street
Healdsburg, California 95448
707-433-1381

The Boonville Hotel
14050 Highway 128
Boonville, California 95415
707-895-2210

Brava Terrace
3010 St. Helena Highway (Hwy. 29)
St. Helena, California 94574
707-963-9300

Cafe Beaujolais
961 Ukiah Street
Mendocino, California 95460
707-937-5614

Catahoula Restaurant and Saloon
1457 Lincoln Avenue
Calistoga, California 94515
707-942-2275

Chateau Souverain – Cafe at the Winery
400 Souverain Road
Geyserville, California 95441
707-433-8281

Domaine Chandon Restaurant
1 California Boulevard
Yountville, California 94599
707-944-2280

Downtown Bakery and Creamery
308A Center Street
Healdsburg, California 95448
707-431-2719

Eastside Oyster Bar and Grill
133 East Napa Street
Sonoma, California 95476
707-939-1266

*The Grille at the Sonoma Mission Inn
and Spa*
18140 Sonoma Highway (Hwy. 12)
Boyes Hot Springs, California 95416
707-938-9000

John Ash and Company
4330 Barnes Road
Santa Rosa, California 95403
707-527-7687

Kenwood Restaurant and Bar
10400 Sonoma Highway (Hwy. 12)
Kenwood, California 95452
707-833-6326

The Ledford House Restaurant
3000 North Highway 1
Albion, California 95410
707-937-0282

Madrona Manor
1001 Westside Road
Healdsburg, California 95448
707-433-4231

The Model Bakery
1357 Main Street
St. Helena, California 94574
707-963-8192

Mustards Grill
7399 St. Helena Highway (Hwy. 29)
Napa, California 94558
707-944-2424

955 Ukiah Street Restaurant
955 Ukiah Street
Mendocino, California 95460
707-937-1955

Ristorante Piatti
405 First Street
Sonoma, California 95476
707-996-2351

The Restaurant at Meadowood
900 Meadowood Lane
St. Helena, California 94574
707-963-3646

Samba Java
109A Plaza Street
Healdsburg, California 95448
707-433-5282

St. Orres
36601 Highway 1
Gualala, California 95445
707-884-3335

Stars Oakville Cafe
7848 St. Helena Highway (Hwy. 29)
Oakville, California 94562
707-944-8905

Terra
1345 Railroad Avenue
St. Helena, California 94574
707-963-8931

Tra Vigne Ristorante
1050 Charter Oak Avenue
(at Highway 29)
St. Helena, California 94574-1316
707-963-4444

Willowside Cafe
3535 Guerneville Road
Santa Rosa, California 95401
707-523-4814

METRIC CONVERSIONS

Liquid Weights

U.S. Measurements	Metric Equivalents
1/4 teaspoon	1.23 ml
1/2 teaspoon	2.5 ml
3/4 teaspoon	3.7 ml
1 teaspoon	5 ml
1 dessertspoon	10 ml
1 tablespoon (3 teaspoons)	15 ml
2 tablespoons (1 ounce)	30 ml
1/4 cup	60 ml
1/3 cup	80 ml
1/2 cup	120 ml
2/3 cup	160 ml
3/4 cup	180 ml
1 cup (8 ounces)	240 ml
2 cups (1 pint)	480 ml
3 cups	720 ml
4 cups (1 quart)	1 litre
4 quarts (1 gallon)	3 3/4 litres

Dry Weights

U.S. Measurements	Metric Equivalents
1/4 ounce	7 grams
1/3 ounce	10 grams
1/2 ounce	14 grams
1 ounce	28 grams
1 1/2 ounces	42 grams
1 3/4 ounces	50 grams
2 ounces	57 grams
3 1/2 ounces	100 grams
4 ounces (1/4 pound)	114 grams
6 ounces	170 grams
8 ounces (1/2 pound)	227 grams
9 ounces	250 grams
16 ounces (1 pound)	464 grams

Temperatures

Fahrenheit	Celsius (Centigrade)
32°F (water freezes)	0°C
200°F	95°C
212°F (water boils)	100°C
250°F	120°C
275°F	135°C
300°F (slow oven)	150°C
325°F	160°C
350°F (moderate oven)	175°C
375°F	190°C
400°F (hot oven)	205°C
425°F	220°C
450°F (very hot oven)	230°C
475°F	245°C
500°F (extremely hot oven)	260°C

Length

U.S. Measurements	Metric Equivalents
1/8 inch	3 mm
1/4 inch	6 mm
3/8 inch	1 cm
1/2 inch	1.2 cm
3/4 inch	2 cm
1 inch	2.5 cm
1 1/4 inches	3.1 cm
1 1/2 inches	3.7 cm
2 inches	5 cm
3 inches	7.5 cm
4 inches	10 cm

Approximate Equivalents

1 kilo is slightly more than 2 pounds
1 litre is slightly more than 1 quart
1 centimeter is approximately 3/8 inch

Agnolotti, duck *confit,* 103

Albion River Inn, 126–29

Allen, Richard, 84

All Seasons Cafe and Wine Shop, 58–61

Anise

-flavored bread rolls, 97; seeds, 107

Apples

baked caramel, with berry sauce, 33; with braised squab, 90; caramelized *clafoutis,* 133; cobbler, 129; tart, with polenta, 101

Apricots, soufflé of dried, 105

Arugula, 25, 59, 64

Ash, John, 88

Auberge du Soleil, 34–37

Avocado butter, 124

Banana sorbet, 23

Beans

black, purée of, 104; *cannellini,* in salad, 64; Chinese fermented black, 94; Great Northern, 39; navy, 132; Soupy White, 132; white, 18

Beef

cheeks, braised, 32; New York strip, seared, 78; skirt steak, grilled, 26

Beets

in salad, 73; soup of roasted, 135

Bell peppers

in catsup, 26; in salad, 73; in salsa, 74; sautéed medley of, 104; in slaw, 63, 89; in soup, 81, 113

Berries, with shortcake, 109

Birnbaum, Jan, 62

Bistro Don Giovanni, 16–19

Bistro Ralph, 96–99

Blackberries

and mango upside-down cake, 65; with shortcake, 109

Blueberry scones, 101

Boonville Hotel, 112–15

Brandy

apple, 133; apricot, 105; in ice cream, 74

Brava Terrace, 54–57

Bread

focaccine, 97; pudding, cappuccino, 37; walnut, 52

Breiman, Roy, 38

Bruschetta, wild mushroom, 77

Butter, avocado, 124

Buttermilk, 73, 101, 109

Cabbage

with braised squab, 90; salad, 48; in slaw, 89, 94

Cafe Beaujolais, 130–33

Cake (*see also* Torte)

butter *(Torta Sabiosa),* 45; chocolate-polenta mousse, 19; flourless chocolate coconut, 61; Jack Daniels, 27; mango and blackberry upside-down, 65; turtle, 51

Calvados, 133

Campiformio, Rosemary, 118

Caramel

and baked apple, 33; sauce

for bread pudding, 37; for poached pears, 71; for turtle cake, 51

Carrot juice, with sea bass, 98

Carrots

baby, 131; in couscous, 108; in salad 73; in slaw, 94; in vegetable purée, 32

Cassoulet, of lentils, with chicken, sausage, and pork, 56

Catahoula Restaurant and Saloon, 62–65

Catsup, pepper, 26

Celery root, in vegetable purée, 32

Chantilly cream, 125

Chard, red, in lasagne, 86

Chateau Souverain, Cafe at the Winery 106–109

Chayote and tomatillo salsa, 74

Cheese

chèvre, 35; cream, 103; fontina, 31, 77; goat, 86

in *involtini,* 69; marinated, 55; salad of, 43, 55; tartlets, 35

mascarpone, 35; Monterey Jack, 74; pecorino, 70; ricotta, sheep's milk, 86; Stilton, 17

Chenel, Laura, 30

Chestnuts

in ragout with mushrooms, 131; with squab, 90; to peel, 131

Chiarello, Michael, 42

Chicken

breast

in cassoulet, 56; with potato and pea risotto, 44; roasted Sonoma, 108

Chile (*see also* Peppers)

Anaheim, 104; *ancho,* 114; *chipotle,* 26; Fresno, 25, 26; *pasilla,* 25, 114; *serrano,* 86, 93, 94; Thai, 93

Chocolate

cake

coffee-flavored, 51; flourless, with coconut, 61; with polenta, 19; with whiskey, 27

mousse, 19; pâté, 99; sorbet, 23; truffle torte, 125; waffles, 79

Cider, apple, 90

Citrus vinaigrette, 123

Clafoutis, caramelized apple, 133

Cobbler, apple-crumb, 129

Coconut, and chocolate cake, 61

Coconut milk, 48, 93

Coffee

in bread pudding, 37; and chocolate cake, 51, 125

Confit

duck, 103; tomato, 64

Cookies

almond, 71; praline, 87

Corn
crêpes, 73, 86; with pork loin, 74; salsa, 104; soup of roasted, 135; in stuffing for *pasillas*, 25

Coulis
raspberry, 82; tomato, 86

Courtman, Martin, 106

Couscous, vegetable, 108

Cranberry kuchen, 115

Cream
Chantilly, 125; English, 56; lemon, for pasta, 103; sauce, hot, 115

Crème anglaise, ginger, 91

Crème brûlée, ginger, 95

Crème fraîche, 87

Crêpes, corn, 73, 86

Croutons, cheese, 55, 77

Curry sauce, Thai red, 48

Daikon sprouts *(kiaware)*, 47

Dierkhising, Mark, 58

Dill, for soup, 107

Domaine Chandon Restaurant, 20–23

Doumaini, Lissa, 46

Downtown Bakery and Creamery 100–101

Dressing, Sonoma mustard, 73 *(see also* Vinaigrette)

Duck
breast, marinated and sautéed, 60 *confit*, 103; roast, lasagne of, 86; stock, 86

Eastside Oyster Bar and Grill, 72–75

Eggplant, *involtini* of, 69

Eggs, quail, 120

Epazote, 132

Fennel, bulbous
roast, 31; in slaw, 63; in soup, 107

Field, Carol, 101

Figs
oven-dried, 43; with raspberry coulis and mint, 82; and raspberry gratin, 87

Fish *(see also* Seafood)
ahi tuna
peppered, 82; and salmon *tempura sushi*, 36; *tataki* of, 47
halibut
in corn crêpes, 86; gravlax of, 123; pan-roasted, 132
salmon
and ahi tuna *tempura sushi*, 36; grilled with avocado butter and fried sage, 124; with cabbage, Thai curry sauce and *basmati* rice, 48; poached, with tomato and tarragon sauce, 136; smoked, 21
sea bass
braised, 98; with lentils and mashed potatoes, 22
trout, smoked red, 21

Focaccine, anise-flavored, 97

Foie gras, with steak, 78

Fox, Margaret, 130

Franz, Mark, 30

Frisée, 17, 21, 43

Fruit, fresh, with English cream and mint, 56

Galangal, 93

Ganache, 51

Garlic
poached, 35; roasted, 78

Gazpacho, 81

Geer, Lisa, 122

Geer, Tony, 122

Ginger
in *crème anglaise*, 91; *crème brûlée*, 95; with kale, 132; in marinade, 128; in orange-Riesling sauce, 127; pickled, 36; in risotto, 127; with sea bass, 98

Gratin, fig and raspberry, 87

Greens, baby salad, 35, 47, 55, 59, 73

Griffith, Jaimie, 134

Griffith, Peggy, 134

Grille at the Sonoma Mission Inn and Spa, The, 76–79

Hale, Carol, 84

Hale, David, 34

Hale, Michael, 84

Halpert, Fred, 54, 57

Hangtown Fry, Eastside's, 73

Horseradish sauce, 78

Huber, Marsha, 50

Huckleberry
sauce, 60, 128, 137; tart, 121

Ice cream
brandy 'n' spice, 75; vanilla-bean, 129

Involtini, with goat cheese, 69

Jeanty, Philippe, 20

John Ash and Company, 88–91

Kaiware (daikon sprouts), 47

Kale, wilted, 132

Kenwood Restaurant and Bar, 80–82

Kuchen, cranberry, 115

Kump, Christopher, 130

Lamb
braised shanks, 18; medallions, 40

Lane, Doug, 68

Lasagne, roast duck, 86

Ledford House Restaurant, The, 122–25

Leek, and potato soup, 107

Lemon
cream, for pasta, 103; vinaigrette, 73

Lemongrass, 93

Lentils, green French, 22, 56

Lynch, Terry, 24

McGlynn, Colleen, 92

Madeira, 77

Madrona Manor, 102–105

Madura, Jeff, 88

Mango
and blackberry upside-down cake, 65 mousse, 137

Maple syrup, 120, 131

Marinade
for chicken, 44; for gravlax of halibut 123; for pork, 128; for skirt steak, 26; for veal loin, 104
Mayonnaise, blood orange, 89
Medley
of peppers, 104; wild rice and pasta, 128
Mitchell, Karen, 50
Model Bakery, The, 50–52
Mousse
chocolate, 19; mango, with huckleberry sauce, 137
Muir, Todd, 102
Mushrooms
in cassoulet, 56; *chanterelle,* 77; oyster, 77, 93; *shiitake,* 36, 77, 86, 128; wild, 120, 131
Mustard dressing, 73
Mustards Grill, 24–27

955 Ukiah Street Restaurant, 134–37
Nori, 36, 119
Nuts
almonds
in cookies, 71, 87; and orange tart, 91; shortcake, 109
hazelnuts, in cookies, 87; peanuts in slaw, 94; pecans in cake, 27; pine in pasta sauce, 70
walnuts
in bread, 52; in cake, 125; candied, 17

Oil
Brazil nut, 59; chile, 74; white truffle, 31
Olives, 70
Onions
green, 63, 89; pearl, 131
red
braised, 32; with medallions of lamb, 40; in salsa, 104; in slaw, 63

yellow
in soup, 81, 113
in couscous, 108
Orange juice, 127
Orange liqueur, and almond tart, 91
Oranges, blood, in mayonnaise, 89

Papaya, with tuna, 82
Pasta
fresh
for *agnolotti,* 103; for lasagne, 86; saffron fettuccine, 119
orzo, with wild rice, 128; pumpkin-filled gratin, 31; saffron, with seafood, 119; Siciliana, 70
Pastry
brik, 40; phyllo, 35, 40, 105; tart, 75, 91, 101, 121
Pâté, chocolate, 99
Pawlcyn, Cindy, 24
Pears
poached
with caramel sauce, 71; and cinnamon vanilla risotto, 41
salad, with Stilton, 17
sorbet, 23
Peas, English, and potato risotto, 44
Pepper, black, with strawberries, 49
Peppers (*see also* Bell peppers; Chiles)
cherry, 104; grilled stuffed *pasilla,* 25; jalapeño, 74, 81, 94, 113, 114; medley of, 104; yellow (hot), 104
Pernod, 97, 132
Pineapple, fresh, with pork loin, 74
Plantains, fried, 94
Plums, Santa Rosa, tart of, 75
Polenta
and apple tart, 101; and chocolate cake, 19
soft
with cheese, 74; with jalapeño, 114
Pork
loin
in cassoulet, 56; house-smoked

128; roast, red chile oregano, 114; spiced, smoked and grilled, 74; spareribs, Chinese black bean, 94
Potatoes
and green pea risotto, 44; and leek soup, 107
mashed, 22
with garlic, 78
with smoked trout, 21
Praline, cookies, 87
Pudding, warm cappuccino bread, 37
Pumpkin
in pasta gratin, 31; soup, with coconut, 93

Quail, wild mushroom-stuffed, 120

Rabbit, warm salad of roasted, 64
Radish
with halibut, 86
Japanese *(daikon),* 73
sprouts *(kiaware),* 47
Ragout, chestnut and wild mushroom, 131
Raspberries
and fig gratin, 87; purée, for cake, 125; sauce, 33, 79, 82; with shortcake, 109
Rémoulade, 63
Restaurant at Meadowood, The, 38–41
Rice
arborio, 41, 133, *basmati,* 48; orzo medley, 128; white, 128; wild, 60
Risotto
cinnamon vanilla, 41; with ginger, 127; potato and pea, 44
Ristorante Piatti, 68–71
Rouas, Claude, 68

Sage, with salmon, 124
St. Orres, 118–21
Salad
cabbage, 48 (*see also* Slaw)
Comice pear and Stilton, 17

goat cheese
    marinated, 55
    with oven-dried figs, 43
  warm rabbit and white bean, 64
  vegetable, 73
Salsa
  corn, 104
  tomatillo, 25;
    and *chayote,* 74
Samba Java, 92–94
Sauce (*see also* Coulis)
  savory
    avocado butter, 124; fall squash, 103;
    horseradish, 78; huckleberry, 60,
    128; Marinara, 69; rémoulade, 63;
    Siciliana 70; Thai red curry, 48;
    tomato and tarragon, 136
  dessert
    berry, 33
    caramel
      for bread pudding, 37; for cake,
      51; for poached pears, 71
    hot cream, 115; huckleberry, 137;
    orange-Riesling cream, 127;
    raspberry, 33, 79, 82
Saunders, Charles, 72
Sausage, 56, 120
Scala, Donna, 16
Scala, Giovanni, 16
Schacher, Maxime, 80
Schacher, Susan, 80
Schmidt, Johnny, 112
Scones, blueberry, 101
Seafood
  calamari, and bean vinaigrette, 39
  crab
    cakes, 89; soft-shell, 63
  crawfish tails, in rémoulade, 63;
  mussels, with pasta, 119
  oysters, in Hangtown Fry 73
  saffron pasta and, 119
  scallops
    with pasta, 119; sesame-seared, 127
  shrimp, with pasta, 119

squid, with pasta, 119
Seaweed (*see Nori*)
Shere, Lindsey, 100
Shortcake, almond, with berries, 109
Slaw
  cabbage, 89 (*see also* Salad, cabbage);
    confetti, 94; vegetable, 63
Smith, Steve, 126
Sone, Hiro, 46
Sorbet
  banana, 23; chocolate, 23; pear, 23
Soufflés, apricot, in phyllo, 105
Soup
  gazpacho, 81; leek and potato, with
    anise, 107; roasted vegetable bisque
    113; roasted white corn and red beet
    135; spicy coconut and pumpkin, 93
Spice, *sushi,* 36
Spice mix
  for chicken, 44; Navaho, 74
Spinach, baby, 44, 89
Squab, braised in cider, 90
Squash, acorn, sauce of, 103
Stars Oakville Cafe, 30–33
Stewart, Kathleen, 100
Stock
  duck, 86; fish, 136; lamb, 40
Strawberries
  for cake topping, 45; sauce, 33;
    sautéed in red wine and black pepper,
    49; with shortcake, 109
Stuffing
  for *pasillas,* 25; for quail, 120
Sushi, ahi and salmon *tempura,* 36

Tarragon, 136
Tart
  almond orange, 91; apple polenta,
    101; Santa Rosa plum, 75; wild
    huckleberry, 121
Tartlets, goat cheese, 35
Tequila, 74
Terra, 46–49

Tingle, Ralph, 96
Tobiko (flying fish roe), 119
Tomatillo salsa, 25
  with *chayote,* 74
Tomatoes
  confit, 64; coulis, 86; sauce, 69; in
    soup, 81, 113; sun-dried, 104, 136;
    and tarragon sauce, 136
Topping
  cobbler, 129; fruit, for cake, 45
Torta Sabiosa, 45
Torte, chocolate truffle, 125
Tower, Jeremiah, 30
Tra Vigne Ristorante, 42–45
Turnips, in vegetable purée, 32

Vann, Mark, 76
Veal, loin steak, 104
Vegetables
  bisque of roasted, 113; couscous, 108;
    root, purée of, 32; slaw, 63
Vinaigrette (*see also* Dressing)
  Brazil nut oil, 59; citrus, 123; garlic
    balsamic, 35; for goat cheese salad,
    55; lemon, 73; mustard-soy, 47;
    pickled ginger, 36; sherry balsamic,
    47; sherry and walnut, 17; white
    bean, 39
Vinegar, balsamic
  reduction of, 64; with strawberries, 45;
    in vinaigrette, 35, 39, 47, 55, 64, 123

Waffles
  warm chocolate, 79; yam, 120
Wasabi, 36
Whiskey, cake, 27
Willowside Cafe, 84–87

Yam
  cakes, with wild rice, 60
  waffles, 120

Zucchini, in slaw, 63